Advance Praise for *The Suburban Church*

"Following God's call and the urging of five brave families, Arthur DeKruyter founded and then built Christ Church of Oak Brook into one of the largest, most vibrant suburban churches in North America. His story is a compelling one, surprisingly understated, as he outlines the lessons he learned and the mistakes he made along the way. Pastors and church leaders who find themselves in suburban settings will want this new book for insight and inspiration."
—Rev. Douglas J. Brouwer, Pastor, First Presbyterian Church, Ann Arbor, Michigan

"The message in *The Suburban Church* is a must-read for believers who care about the church, the urban or suburban, especially if they are church builders. Art DeKruyter shares it because he did it."
—Rich DeVos, Cofounder of Amway and Owner of the Orlando Magic

"DeKruyter provides significant insights that can help churches and leaders reach the American suburban culture with the love of Christ. Take it from someone who has 'been there and done that' successfully."
—Peter Semeyn, Senior Pastor, Faith Reformed Church, Traverse City, Michigan

"In addition to his authenticity, fairness, loyalty, and other outstanding leader characteristics, what impressed me the most about Art DeKruyter in the nineteen years I served with him at Christ Church of Oak Brook is his principled procedure in decision making. Consistently in our staff meeting deliberations he would lift up before us the relevant biblical, theological, and philosophical principles that would, together with the Holy Spirit's help for which we prayed at the beginning of the meetings, enable us to construct the most effective approach to the issues before us. Those key principles and the ways in which he facilitated their application in founding and building the church are in this book."
—Rev. Edward D. Seely, PhD

The Suburban Church

The Suburban Church

Practical Advice for Authentic Ministry

Arthur H. DeKruyter

with

Quentin J. Schultze

Westminster John Knox Press
LOUISVILLE • LONDON

Book design by Sharon Adams
Cover design by Lisa Buckley
Cover photo: © *Ron Chapple/Corbis*

First edition
Published by Westminster John Knox Press
Louisville, Kentucky

This book is printed on acid-free paper that meets the American National Standards Institute Z39.48 standard. ♾

PRINTED IN THE UNITED STATES OF AMERICA

08 09 10 11 12 13 14 15 16 17 — 10 9 8 7 6 5 4 3 2 1

Library of Congress Cataloging-in-Publication Data

DeKruyter, Arthur H.
   The suburban church : practical advice for authentic ministry / Arthur H. DeKruyter ; with Quentin J. Schultze. — 1st ed.
       p. cm.
     ISBN 978-0-664-23294-8 (alk. paper)
     1. Suburban churches. 2. Church work. I. Schultze, Quentin J. (Quentin James), 1952– II. Title.

   BV637.7.D45 2008
   250.9173'3—dc22

                                                            2007041811

Dedicated to the memory of my wife, Gladys,
the visionary who encouraged me to seize opportunities,
kept me spiritually alert and alive,
whose prayers still uphold me,
my lifelong friend and love.

Contents

Foreword

Bethany was Jesus' favorite suburb. He often commuted the 1.8 miles into the city of Jerusalem where much of his ministry took place. Bethany was home to three of his best friends—Mary, Martha, and Lazarus. Jesus ate there, slept there, and performed his top miracle in Bethany when he brought Lazarus out of the grave alive.

The term *suburb* can be misleading. When dissected, it means under ("sub") the city ("urb"), but that tells us very little. The word comes from the historical domination of little towns by big cities. Cities are the center; cities are where the action is; cities are important; cities dominate. Suburbs are underneath. The everyday understanding is that cities are in the center and suburbs are around the perimeter.

The Metro-Donut

Once upon a time, the cities were where the rich and powerful lived in mansions while the poor and weak lived out of town where housing was cheap. In twentieth-century America that notion was turned inside out, and many thought of the city as the center of poverty and disenfranchisement while the suburbs were loaded with the rich and influential. At the beginning of the twenty-first century, many metropolitan areas are reversing the donut one more time. Center cities are booming with lofts and condos filled with empty-nest baby boomers, rich and sophisticated young adults, and the urban elite, who love the downtown ambiance and consider suburbs to be sterile and bland. At the same time, first- and second-generation immigrant families are coloring once-white suburbs as they seek bigger houses and better schools.

Suburbs are not what they used to be. Some are huge. By comparison, first-century Athens had a population around 10,000. That would be a small suburb by twenty-first-century standards. Some of today's megasuburbs are home to hundreds of thousands of people. Most American cities have a smaller population within the city limits than the combined population of the surrounding suburbs. Then there are large urban corridors reaching from Washington to Boston that function as an integrated matrix of urban and suburban where only the local residents can tell where one town ends and the next begins.

So what does all this mean for church ministry in twenty-first-century American suburbs?

Suburbs Are Communities

Suburbs are communities with distinct identities and clear boundaries. Just as New Yorkers identify with the urban distinctives of Brooklyn or the Bronx, in nearby New Jersey residents identify with the suburbs of Jersey City and Montclair. We all need to break down the large scale into more personal and manageable units.

Church leaders must become demographers and ethnographers who know the difference between Oak Brook and Elmhurst, between Pasadena and Altadena. When Arthur DeKruyter started Christ Church with a small cadre of Christians, he analyzed Oak Brook and customized the church's ministry to fit the people and place. Had he tried to fit his experiences from another town it would have been a formula for failure. Instead, understanding the affluent and influential character of Oak Brook became a formula for success. Not that this formula will work elsewhere. Other church leaders must follow the principles but adapt the practices. Every suburb is different, and every church must customize to its own community.

Stewardship of Suburbia

There is no shortage of books and movies critical of suburban life and culture. Some have a prejudice against suburbs expressed in angry pejorative terms. They draw a caricature of suburbs and suburban churches as wealthy, isolated, ethnocentric, mono-cultural, selfish, materialistic, and morally flawed. This is itself an uninformed and ethnocentric prejudice.

People choose to live in communities for thousands of different reasons. I know a suburban neighborhood where many of the houses have been purchased by young families because either the husband or wife grew up in that neighborhood. They have happy memories and want to pass their happiness on to their children. Others choose to live in a suburb because of proximity to employment, because of schools, because the suburb is where they can afford to live, or because it is halfway between the homes of grandparents. And yes, there are some who prefer gated communities to keep unlike people out, but one shouldn't stereotype all residents as sharing similar motives.

The same can be said of urban communities where residents have come because of proximity to a large university, downtown theaters, ethnic and language background, or public transportation.

Churches should celebrate the resources of the communities they serve and call each congregation to stewardship of their local distinctives. Near a large urban university there is huge intellectual capital to be used for the kingdom of Jesus Christ. In a largely Hispanic or Hmong neighborhood there is ethnicity and heritage that can be leveraged for Jesus. In a wealthy and influential suburb there is a deep reservoir of resources to benefit and bless others. Rather than compare or criticize, one should celebrate and capitalize on the blessings God has given to each community.

Specifically, a church near a major university can penetrate

American intelligentsia far better than a small farm town. The church in a black immigrant community will be far more effective in evangelizing recent arrivals from West Africa or Somalia than a downtown, mostly white region of high-rise condominiums. And an affluent suburban congregation outside of Phoenix or Philadelphia can give far more money to fight HIV-AIDS in a developing nation than a church in a dying southeastern cotton mill town.

So, yes, some suburbs are disproportionately rich and powerful. The biblical challenge is to use that money and power for the cause of Christ and the needs of people. That is the story of Christ Church Oak Brook. Arthur DeKruyter analyzed the Chicago suburb, developed the strategies described in this book, and fulfilled the biblical call of Jesus Christ in a ministry that reached people of Oak Brook, greater Chicago, and around the world. What can be learned? What can be applied to other suburbs and congregations?

DeKruyter is a mentor for suburban pastors and church leaders. A mentor is someone we get to know so well that we can predict how that person would behave in a situation he has never been in. In other words, read and learn about Arthur DeKruyter and Christ Church as a case study. Get into his head—philosophy, theology, decision making, spiritual values—until you know what he would do in your suburb and your church.

Looking Ahead

Those who live and lead in an early-twenty-first-century suburb want to know what to expect as we move into the 2010s, 2020s, and 2030s.

Suburbs will be older. America is aging and millions of Americans are aging in place. While some retire to Florida and Arizona in their sixties, they are a reverse migration in their eighties when octogenarians return to their hometowns nearer adult children and grandchildren. The median age of Americans is 35.3 years, the oldest in the nation's history.[1] And 76 million baby boomers

---

1.   http://usgovinfo.about.com/library/weekly/aa051801a.htm

born between 1946 and 1964 will soon swell the ranks of senior adults and retirees. Not that there won't be new subdivisions in rapidly growing states like Nevada and Arizona, but older suburbs with older houses, older people, and older churches will outnumber the new. Established churches will need to reinvent themselves to reach a changing and aging clientele.

More people will be alone. In 1940 fewer than 8 percent of Americans lived alone. Today nearly 26 percent live alone. Suburban churches that flourished with young families living in four bedroom colonials will increasingly minister to single adults in every age category. This complicates ministry because the congregation of three hundred used to relate to 100 households and now relates to 150 or 200 households. Lonely people are reached in different ways and may be more difficult to reach.

Diversity will abound. One of the stereotypes is that suburbs are highly homogeneous—almost all the residents look alike, act alike, and reside in tract homes with similar floor plans. The homogeneity of suburbs is rapidly changing. While cities have often had neighborhoods organized around ethnicity, race, or socioeconomic class, suburbs are increasingly diverse. To put it another way, suburbs mix up the population while many cities concentrate populations. Expect to see suburbs with more races, more languages, more mixed marriages, more same-gender couples, and more lifestyles than ever before. Churches will become more like local ecclesiastical United Nations in contrast to the harsh stereotype of an earlier generation, for whom "eleven o'clock Sunday morning [was] the most segregated hour of the American week."

More churches will be needed. Some churches birthed in the twentieth century will go out of ministry—the people will grow too old, the building will become too worn, and the cost to survive will be too high. Some churches will adapt to changing demographics, worship styles, and culture and flourish. And thousands of new congregations will begin. When the post–World War II suburban expansion began to boom in 1950, the population of the United States was 161,325,798.[2] In 2007 the population reached 300 million and is on its way to a projected 400 million by 2043.[3] There are varying estimates of the number of congregations in America and the ratio of churches to people. Most say that there are more churches than a century ago but not close to the number needed to serve the increased population. To just keep up there should be twice as many churches as there are. We need an army of Arthur DeKruyters who will pioneer new churches to reach people that are unserved or underserved by existing churches.

As the Suburbs Go

An old political adage claimed that "as Maine goes, so goes the nation." It has been modified a multitude of times. As for churches and Christianity, many would claim that "as the cities go, so goes the nation." Equally arguable is that "as the suburbs go, so goes the nation." Suburban churches can and do influence America. This will increase as the calendar turns deeper into the twenty-first century. Suburban churches can and should reach millions of people, disciple generations of Christians, steward billions of dollars, parent tens of thousands of new congregations, and advance the gospel of Jesus Christ in the hundreds of nations on our earth.

Arthur DeKruyter and Christ Church give us the story of this book. May there be many more.

Leith Anderson

2.   http://www.u-s-history.com/pages/h980.html
3.   http://www.cnn.com/2006/US/10/17/300.million.over/index.html

Acknowledgments

After years of association in ministry of Christ Church, I learned to respect the judgment of my colleague who dedicated his life to the study and development of the educational obligation of the Church of Jesus Christ. Dr. Edward Seely, educator, lecturer, seminary professor, and research director, urged me to write a book about our experiences. It is with great appreciation for his persistent encouragement that this project is now completed.

When Dr. Quentin Schultze, expert in the field of communication arts and sciences and nationally recognized voice in the mainstream media, offered to help the project as consultant and editor, I was elated. This had to be providence at work. I am deeply indebted to him not only for his expertise but for his dedication to the integrity of the book, our personal friendship, and our mutual effort to make a humble but deliberate attempt to bring honor to the Church of Jesus Christ.

I must also give public thanksgiving for the continuous flow of love and support in the congregation of Christ Church of Oak Brook. Typical of that spiritual journey was the help of one of the members in making this book a reality. Special recognition is due to Marjorie Samec, who patiently and meticulously deciphered and transcribed my pitiable handwritten manuscript, and to Kim Chimienti, who served Dr. Schultze as editorial assistant.

Introduction

My forty-five years of pastoral ministry came to an end with a great Friday evening celebration. I had spent the last thirty-one years planting and nurturing Christ Church of Oak Brook in suburban Chicago. Now colleagues and friends compressed my ministry into a video documentary. The large congregation affirmed the blessings that they, my wife, Gladys, and I enjoyed in this remarkable community of faith.

But it was still difficult to accept all of the congratulations, since it was obvious to attendees that the Lord had led us all the way. By God's grace, a core group of five couples had called me as a young pastor to this suburban church plant in the early 1960s. Three decades later, it was clear that neither the founding couples nor their young pastor had ever dreamed of what God was preparing for us—both the blessings and the challenges. The celebration reflected the words of the apostle Paul to the church at Ephesus: we had become God's workmanship, "created in Christ Jesus for good works, which God prepared beforehand to be our way of life" (Eph. 2:10).

That night we gratefully recalled the fruit: a church campus with a 1,200-seat sanctuary and adequate building and equipment for our 5,000 members; three healthy services each Sunday morning that regularly drew people from over 130 suburbs and the city of Chicago; twelve trustees and ninety elders who led the congregation with the support of a dedicated, competent staff; excellent adult, youth, and children's education programs; special ministries in music, counseling, and preschool; and outreach programs supporting over fifty missionaries as well as domestic, inner-city, and international ministries.

This book is not just the story of my ministry or of Christ Church of Oak Brook. Instead it is a practical, discerning guide to principles behind planting, growing, and leading a suburban church in North America. I explain how the suburbs are increasingly fertile soil for growing churches that are *incarnational* (based on strong, relational, localized ministry), *indigenous* (growing out of specific suburban culture), *historic* (premised on ancient biblical, theological, and even confessional Christian faith), and *intentional* (carefully as well as creatively developed from core beliefs as well as a solid biblical vision).

My examples from Christ Church of Oak Brook are adaptable "parables," not strict methods. I explain the principles behind the many successful and some not-so-effective aspects of our congregation's ministry so that other churches can adapt those principles to their own situations. Moreover, my lifelong experience gives a reader a clear sense of how congregations can adapt the principles over time to the suburban cultures in which they serve.

Each of the chapters addresses a particularly important aspect of suburban ministry, such as how to understand suburban culture, make wise staffing decisions, fit historic preaching and worship to suburban needs and expectations, finance church programs, recruit and train gifted volunteers, and nurture spiritual maturity among members of all ages. Established congregations as well as new suburban churches will find this book helpful as they continually adapt ministry to unfolding opportunities and unexpected setbacks. Clearly suburbs will continue to be where the majority of North Americans live, so the church needs to be there, listening and learning from suburbanites as well as missionally working with them on the task of being faithful where God has planted them.

Chapter One

Listening in the Suburbs

One astonishing phone call shook up my comfortable life as pastor of a growing suburban church. My family was even more stunned. "How could you leave your church to go off with five families to do such a foolish thing?" my seventy-seven-year-old father exclaimed when I proposed to depart my beloved congregation and start a new church from scratch. His words wore on my anxious soul. I loved and deeply respected my father. I wanted to listen to him and to take his concern seriously.

Suburban Churches and Restaurants

I *was* a bit crazy. Any group that starts a new suburban church or tries to revive a dying one is somewhat daffy. Most church plants and turnarounds fail. They burn out pastors and laity alike. They even become huge financial drains on denominations and often on a few key families for whom the weekly tithes begin to look like bad stock market investments.

Suburban churches seem like restaurants. They come and go with new "owners" and menus, hoping to capitalize on trends. Or they fail to adapt to changing neighborhood "clientele" and slowly wither away. Like churches, restaurants involve extensive relationship-building, community-serving, taxing work that seems endless.

Both require a large staff, although in churches the staff are primarily volunteers. Then there are the long hours, unexpected setbacks, fussy customers, and all the rest.

Suburban ministry can be especially deceptive. Most young ministers see suburban pastoring as relatively easy or at least comfortable. The pay is better than rural ministry. Living conditions are easier than with much urban ministry and probably at most foreign missions posts. The area schools and civic clubs are relatively well funded. Unless embroiled in internal conflict, suburban congregations appear to be the most hospitable venues for ministry.

Laity, too, view suburban churches as relatively easy. They generally think that the pastor will do most of the work. Some members, based on their own professional success, think that a suburban church is an opportunity for them to fashion the congregation in their own image of "success." Even with the best of motives, they can be controlling and impatient with clergy and volunteers. They forget that every local congregation already has a reputation in its community and that such reputations are not easy to improve. Customers who were poorly served a bad meal are not likely to return to the same restaurant!

Nevertheless, the suburbs are expanding, like a carpet into the plains, valleys, and hills that surround large and medium-sized cities from coast to coast. For good or for bad, the suburbs are part of North America. So denominations, independent groups, pastors, lay leaders, and hangers-on tread on those rolling carpets in hopes of building a spiritual home amidst strip malls, road construction, and manicured lawns—usually until the neighborhood no longer meets people's expectations and they run after the carpet that has long since rolled along to a new area.

Suburbs Are Not All Alike

Why do so many new suburban churches never take root? Fail to flourish? Grow and then decline? One major reason is a lack of understanding of the diversity of suburban cultures. Denominations often conduct sterile demographic studies that fail to address the local culture. Seminars teach the latest church-planting and church-growth strategies as if one size fits all. Enthusiastic young ministers often start "mission" churches right out of seminary without adequate education in cultural understanding. Optimistic believers band together to launch congregations, hoping to create something new or better than they had previously, but often their optimism turns into frustration because standardized church growth and congregational renewal programs are not adapted to local, indigenous cultures.

The problem is that technique and planning, youthfulness and energy, and desires for change are never themselves adequate. Suburbs, which are mission fields in their own right, need church leaders and members who are wise as well as innovative. The suburbs are not generic places any more than ministers are all the same persons. Every location has its distinct potential and problems—as does every congregation and pastor. Suburban parishes are no exception, even if many of the neighborhoods look alike on the outside.

When I took over the pastorate of an existing suburban church as my first charge, I learned immediately that this collection of saints had its own quirks and talents. In many cases, the people who worshiped in that church were baptized or married there; they were special individuals who comprised a congregation with a unique personality. They were largely Dutch people, many first-generation. Although they were generally frugal, they also tended to be remarkably generous. They did not want sentimental worship or semibiblical preaching. They enjoyed singing psalms—even expected to do so. They stalwartly supported Christian day school and church education. Most were working class. And once upon a time, they had started a suburban church as they moved outward from their ethnic neighborhood. Regardless of why they moved, they had felt called years earlier to start a new church closer to their homes. Over time, that congregation had become theirs, with its own ways of doing ministry. The problem was that the "new" ways had become "old" ways, frequently without meaning or purpose. They were aliens in the surrounding suburban culture, able to minister only to themselves.

Where Christians Are Aliens or Exiles

Peter (1 Peter 2) writes about holy, covenant people who are defined by Christ's call. He says such holy people are aliens who came from another place; their loyalties are foreign, and they seem to possess a strange source of strength. He calls them "exiles." My experience shows that suburban believers are exilic people, too. People come to the suburbs from the city, or at least from other suburbs. Few call their suburban neighborhood their lifelong home.

Over half of all Americans now live in suburbs, with the remainder roughly split between urban and rural locations. Suburbs represent the fastest population growth as well as vast financial and professional resources for Christian causes. Often new denominational headquarters and seminary campuses are located in the expanding population rings around North American cities.

Sociologists coined the term "boomburbs" to describe America's fastest-growing suburban cities and corridors—the areas where housing, industry, commerce, and even small pockets of agricultural land exist practically side by side. Boomburbs have included Scottsdale, Arizona; Naperville, Illinois; and Bellevue, Washington. Scottsdale alone grew nearly 2,000 percent between 1960 and 2000. Over 100 boomburbs have become the focus of church growth among evangelical and recently mainline churches.

Still, the suburbs sometimes seem far removed from a heavenly dwelling place on earth. They can become lamentable places littered with strip malls, ugly housing tracts, stark cement highways carrying noisy traffic, and mobile populations seemingly indifferent to the good of the local community. Two books—*Death by Suburb: How to Keep the Suburbs from Killing Your Soul* and *The Suburban Christian: Finding Spiritual Vitality in the Land of Plenty*—make these points well even if they overstate their cases.

Yet knee-jerk criticisms of the suburbs as places of spiritual exile are just as stereotypical as those of rural or urban America. Jim Wallis of *Sojourners* wrote pejoratively of the "comfortable" suburbanites in contrast to the faithful believers who live the gospel on the streets of Philadelphia, Calcutta, and Iraq. He overlooked the problems that plague many suburban communities, from anxiety and depression to alcoholism, marital infidelity, and sheer meaninglessness. He also implied that suburban Christians are largely Republicans whose self-interested political loyalties have been made "into an almost doctrinal litmus test." Wallis failed to mention that suburban churches and individual suburbanites frequently provide the funding for social causes, including urban and international missions.

Suburbs, like most areas, are a mixed bag of seemingly Christian and non-Christian culture. They are both comfortable dwelling places and seemingly alien lands that make it hard to form deep spiritual communities. In short, suburbs are important mission fields in their own right. To borrow a phrase from Neil Cole's *Organic Church: Growing Where Life Happens*, the church should go "where people congregate," whether in Starbucks or at the local health club. Believers might not feel completely at home in the suburbs, but the same sense of exile exists for Christians everywhere.

Lauren Winner helpfully suggests in a review essay titled "God of the Latte" that suburbanites need to figure out how to learn to "consume more Christianly" by renewing suburban life in tune with the gospel. Albert Hsu says in an interview about his book *The Suburban Christian* that "God needs Christians in suburbia just like he needs Christians everywhere."* He discerningly advocates a recovery of the "parish concept" in suburban church ministry. If suburbs are a kind of spiritual wilderness, they are also places where aliens can rediscover faith and faithful community life.

---

*"Author Interview: Albert Y. Hsu," InterVarsity Press, http://www.ivpress .com/spotlight/3334.php (accessed October 17, 2007).

Specific People, Definite Location, Particular Time

It's hard to imagine the apostle Paul in today's suburban parish, since he was so nonconformist in attitude, appearance, and probably ministry style! But many of his journeys and letters were to congregations in economically advantaged areas that prospered under Roman protection and laws. Paul did not stick around to pastor churches, yet God gave him the wisdom to be all things to all people even under exile to persecution and suffering (2 Cor. 12). He repeatedly applied the gospel creatively to particular people in particular places. In today's world, he probably would have planted suburban churches, recruited faithful persons to lead those churches, and then encouraged and admonished the resulting congregations.

The five couples who called me to start a church in Oak Brook were like Paul's first recruits. They had become concerned for the spiritual lives of the families moving into a community designed for executive suburban living. In late 1964, a magazine insert in the *Chicago Sunday Tribune* featured the community's spacious lots and luxury homes, international sports core (polo, fox hunts, golf, and an air strip), prestigious shopping mall, high-rise executive office spaces, prime access to downtown Chicago, an international airport, and adjacency to three major states. The same article touted the sound economic and cultural benefits of the area but said nothing about resident's spiritual needs. Supposedly suburban heaven on earth had no need for faith. Like ancient Corinth, Oak Brook and environs did not seem to need the gospel.

In my experience, however, some people do move to the suburbs, even to particular suburbs, for the churches. More important to most incoming residents, however, are schools, safety, shopping, and access to commuter highways. Suburban churches follow suburban development—not the other way around. Congregations always seem to be playing catch-up in new, shifting suburban communities.

These five church-planting couples were stunned at what was

happening. How could a "model" village reflect Americans' typical values and religious history without considering congregational life? I agreed that something needed to be done. So with a great sense of being sent by Christ, they urged me to help plant a church. They said that they were willing to work for it. They would volunteer to teach and to tell their neighbors. They were willing to finance it. They, too, were willing to risk for it. Why? Because they believed that the new village could become a community where the love of Christ was present for all. And so these five couples met together to pray and talk with me about these things. Convinced that God was calling us together, we all agreed to move ahead.

Moving Ahead

Our vision was simple. We sought to serve our particular community, not merely to plant a church. Our purpose was broadly biblical, attuned to the early-church concept of growing an organized community of believers where none existed previously. The fact that so many others in the area felt the same way convinced us to move ahead even without the benefit of a building or the legitimacy of a denomination. We felt accountable first to God, who was calling us together; second, to those whom he called to join our budding movement; and finally to the broader community that was increasingly aware of our existence as we worshiped weekly in a neighborhood school gymnasium.

Suburbs support active gossip networks. Residents began talking about our school-based worship services and our vision for serving the community. Visitors came to every service and sometimes to planning meetings as well. It seemed like there was no turning back. Failure would embarrass us and the Lord. It seemed like all we could do was move ahead, working hard to be a friendly, hospitable, faithful new congregation.

By continually listening to and learning from the people whom we sought to serve, we began learning how to reach out to our own "indigenous" suburban culture.

Connecting with a New Culture

Hoping to learn how to connect with our community, I took a course on persuasion at the graduate program in speech at Northwestern University. One of our assignments was to give an eight-minute persuasive talk to a group of people who represented a segment of society different from our backgrounds. Persuasion, we learned, depends on identification between the communicator and the listener. The professor asked those of us in the class a profoundly simple but unnerving question: Had we ever spoken in such a way that others could identify with us?

I decided to rewrite a failed message I had given at the Helping Hand Mission on Chicago's skid row. The more I worked at the speech the more I understood why I had originally botched that sermon. I had prepared a message designed to speak to particular middle-class people like myself, not to those at the mission. I had really spoken to myself, not to those I supposedly was called to serve.

Dr. Edward L. R. Elson, former chaplain of the United States Senate, taught me the same truth. He suggested that a parish preacher sit in the pew of the empty sanctuary on a weekday and pray for parishioners while imagining how they would be feeling during the upcoming Sunday sermon. Get to know those to whom you speak, he emphasized. Listen to them, not to yourself or to other ministers or church experts. If you listen to *them*, they will in turn listen to *you*. Of course the same is true for every Christian and every church. Do believers listen to those they seek to serve?

As I learned during our church development work, many suburban adults feel that no one cares about them because few of their friends, families, and neighbors take the time to listen to them. They feel that Christians talk *at* them, not *with* or *for* them. And they wonder if local churches really care about their aching hearts. They see the televangelists asking for money or visit a church where no one personally acknowledges their presence.

By contrast, Jesus listened on earth for thirty years before he began his ministry. He learned the idioms and habits of the day to illustrate his lessons. He was able to debate the religious leaders by quoting their prophets and poets. He could reach out to farmers and fisherman, mothers and tax collectors, prostitutes and lepers. He would have done the same with suburbanites, identifying with them and speaking to them in the midst of their needs. Sometimes he would have challenged their arrogance, too, or their complacency, self-righteousness, or materialism.

The apostle Paul adapted his messages for very different audiences. The Greeks on Mars Hill (Acts 17) would not have been able to relate to the message he gave to King Agrippa (Acts 26). Theologians tend to think of Paul as a theologian, but those who lead churches should see him as a culturally tuned communicator. Even for pastors who have been raised in the suburbs, and for families that wish to plant churches there, the question remains valid: Can you really identify with the people?

Our biblical agenda was to learn by listening and then to love by serving. Missionaries know that you have to get to know the community, build authentic trust, and avoid arrogant ethnocentrism. Similarly, we needed to win a hearing in our upper-middle-class suburb by tuning in to our neighbors' fears and anxieties as well as their hopes and accomplishments. By listening we discovered that external prosperity often masked spiritual poverty. Affluence and business hid deep self-doubt, addictions, failing relationships, and family turmoils.

Conclusion

I had listened to my father's and others' concerns about me leaving my own denomination to start a community church. But I had also listened to the five couples who called me to serve a churchless community. In the end, my sense of being called by God to their community convinced me to learn with them how to plant and grow a suburban church.

As we listened, we learned. We were coming to understand the community we felt called to serve. With such understanding came empathy. Could we understand and empathize enough that we could begin to serve—to love—a particular people in a particular time and place?

Discussion Questions

1. How can you go about listening to your community? How are you already doing it? How can you do it better?
2. If you are already an organized church, what is the community saying about you?
3. What seem to be the three strongest felt needs among members of your suburban community—what worries them the most? If you cannot answer this question, how will you go about trying to determine the answer?

Chapter Two

Serving the Local Community

Barbara was skeptical about churches. But like many other suburban parents she was increasingly alienated from her children, who seemed to live in their own subculture. Barbara was not ready to attend, let alone join, our church, but she was concerned enough about the so-called "generation gap" between parents and teenagers that with the encouragement of one of our members who was her neighbor, she agreed to host a meeting on the topic at her home.

The resulting cocktail party of nine couples sipped Bloody Marys and smoked cigarettes while I tried to explain to these well-educated suburbanites some of the relativistic ideas and cultural trends that were sweeping intellectuals and youth alike. To my amazement, a lively, unencumbered discussion ensued. I quickly realized how open they were to important, lively discourse. They did not hide from a sensitive issue or merely posture themselves as if everything was fine in their families. In some respects, the discussion seemed easier with these unchurched residents than with Christians I knew who appeared to be either excessively reserved or naively Pollyannaish about the real world.

As a result of this gathering, Barbara enrolled her two sons in our Sunday school program. It took a while, but a number of the attendees eventually attended Christ Church. Some even became members. Moreover, the meeting prompted numerous discussions with other neighborhood parents, leading to more home meetings on similar topics. These sessions generated a remarkably positive reputation for our church throughout the community. Word of mouth began describing me and our church as caring, knowledgeable, and helpful.

Addressing Felt Needs

There are always relevant suburban problems that cry out for answers. The generation gap might not have been equally attractive to urban, ethnic, or rural areas, but it was one of the felt issues simmering in our suburban context. Neighbors had already been talking freely about this issue across backyard fences and while waiting in line at the supermarket. They knew that their children were growing up in a different cultural climate with fewer taboos and perhaps greater cynicism. They were concerned about their own and their children's materialism, drug use, alcohol abuse, marital and generational conflicts, and emotional stress and fatigue.

Every suburban community knows its own problems. Residents hear about each others' health issues. For instance, they see the impact of aging on each others' faces and might be discussing privately their attempts to look younger for as long as possible. They might wonder about where to discover real meaning in life and where to find trusted friends who live authentically in the midst of such personal messes. A wife who discovers that her successful husband is having an affair often wants to know what to do, whom to talk with, how to deal with the entire situation. A husband who loses his corporate job at midcareer contemplates downward mobility and might not want to admit his dilemma to his spouse and certainly not to his children or neighbors; the news seems too embarrassing. What should he do? Whom can he talk with confidentially?

These kinds of topics do come up in small-group conversations, which are a critically important part of suburban social networks. Men are less likely to share their fears and concerns with other men, let alone women beyond their spouses. But they do talk about such matters in general terms while enjoying a backyard picnic with friends and neighbors. Women are more likely to reveal their hearts' concerns to other women, but when the news in their own lives is devastating or embarrassing, they, too, are not sure where to turn. The one major venue for such difficult conversations is when suburbanites gather in someone's home for food, drink, and conversation. We tapped into that network.

The same hostess, Barbara, expressed a greater interest in the faith. So I offered to teach a "Basic Christianity" course informally in her home. Because of her civic involvement and her contagious enthusiasm, she was able to gather together a large number for the twelve-week course. Her rising interest and fine hospitality thereby opened another opportunity for our church to serve. Within a year, members of my church and their neighbors had identified three more homes in which I was welcome to teach the basic course. Later this new course content became a major building block in our on-site church education program. The sessions also spawned many lasting friendships.

How did we persuade people who were not church members to hold these meetings in their homes? We just asked ourselves how we might gain a hearing among this suburban population. How could we serve them where they were—in their homes and lives? All we really needed to do was keep our eyes and ears open for possible hosts who were already asking the kinds of faith-related questions that we could address.

We assumed that authentic, interpersonal, even risky communication about spiritual matters was the best way to interact with our suburbanites, who probably had previously attended churches, perhaps watched disappointing religious television, and for whatever reasons had grown disinterested if not skeptical about the religious establishment. Our observations led us to theorize that these home groups were the best venue for listening to and teaching our suburban neighbors. Expecting them to attend our church without first knowing a bit more about us—and probably something about who Jesus really is—seemed to us to be relatively naïve.

When the apostle Paul went to the city of Athens (cf. Acts 17), he first observed and listened in order to gain an understanding of his audience. What were they thinking and doing? Who were they worshiping? What were the most popular ideas—and who were the leaders that were addressing such ideas? Paul formulated a message related to the existing discussions and topics. He located leaders who had already displayed some interest in the deepest questions of life when they dedicated a statue to the "unknown god." These two steps—determining felt needs and identifying who would listen to us—became our strategy.

Gaining a Hearing with and in the Media

If we were correct about these suburbanites, sending out formal publicity releases and canvassing the neighborhood with brochures about the church would not be adequate. These residents received all kinds of pitches for one activity or another. Yet as we engaged in informal, home-based discussions with interested persons, we realized that we could reinforce our existing interpersonal dialogue with mass-mediated messages. Moreover, we might be able to win over the local media so they would report sympathetically about our community-based ministry.

Our most available means of reaching the villagers was the local newspaper, which was widely read, especially by opinion leaders. (In our case, several papers distributed to our suburb, so we had multiple venues.) Entry-level reporters, usually assigned to the lowly religion pages except during Christmas and Easter seasons, were eager for interesting material to fill their columns. I prepared an article about our opening worship service at the school, accurately describing our vision and goals. Then I hand-delivered it to each newspaper editorial office in an effort to become personally acquainted with the person who managed each one's religion department. Thereafter, we sent weekly updates to each paper. We also occasionally ran a paid advertisement in each paper to enhance our relationship with the staff.

We stated in simple, straightforward language, without hyperbole or trendy lingo, the suburban relevance of the six areas of congregational emphasis that we promised to pursue: worship, music, education, youth, counseling and care, and missions. We developed the stories thematically, offering to suburbanites reasons to watch us as we grew.

Writing and later reading these news-like articles in the paper helped us to remember that we had to be true to our public word—that we had better not create a public image about ourselves that we could not fulfill. When we said that we were going to care for the community, we had to mean it. When we said that our worship services would bless those who attended, we needed to make sure we were a blessing. When we offered to educate in the faith anyone from the community, including his or her children, we had to offer classes that would do so. In a sense, public accountability was built into the structure of our church outreach. If we failed to practice our faith in tune with our PR, we would look no better than any organization that takes advantage of its community's trust. On the other hand, if worship visitors and home-discussion-group attendees discovered that our actions matched our professed beliefs, we would enhance our credibility.

Telling the Tribal and Gospel Stories

As I conducted home discussions and church classes, participating church members and I used the opportunities to tell the "tribal" story of our congregation's calling to Oak Brook. Sharing the story of our church also generated listeners' interest in the gospel. Residents wanted to know why we were serving them—why we cared about them and not just our "church." We had to be ready to offer the reason for our faithful service.

So we discovered opportunities to believe the biblical message and become disciples of Christ. In other words, we tied our tribal story to the gospel, inviting suburbanites to join not just our community but the historic community of all believers. Because it is not always easy to gain a clear picture of where someone stands in his or her relationship to God, such appropriateness was critically important. If visitors indicated an interest in joining our church, however, they had to come "voluntarily" to our "inquirers" classes. This way we could get to know them better and, as appropriate, lead them to Jesus rather than just to church membership.

After the first several months of meeting in the school, it occurred to us that we did not need to organize an evangelism committee. The entire congregation had become the evangelism committee! Our enthusiastic members were bringing friends to worship. They were already discussing their new congregation with non-Christians and with Christians who lacked church homes. Clearly they were motivated by the Spirit of Pentecost. To them, there were stories to tell.

Worship services make the greatest initial impression on the majority of potential church members. That was why worship was our greatest communication-related concern. What "story" did our worship convey to visitors? For those unfamiliar with other parts of worship, preaching and music were the two most compelling components. Our first part-time staff person was a gifted musician who understood how music can and should be used well in worship.

More than any other regular congregational activities, our worship services filled the gymnasium on Sunday mornings and soon prompted us to consider erecting a fitting building. We could always rent space for temporary classrooms and offices, but *where* and *how* we conducted worship were important public statements about our beliefs. The need to serve the community with vibrant worship in a fitting venue seemed to be leading us to build a worship-specific structure, for there were no existing church buildings for us to purchase or rent.

Crowded facilities create building programs, whereas building programs rarely attract crowds. Denominational boards often mistakenly plant churches by erecting a small, seemingly unimportant and often multipurpose facility that neither captures the local congregational vision effectively nor suggests that the local planters are really committed to staying in and growing with the surrounding community. Suburbia is not usually excited or attracted by such constricting ideas. Our suburbanites, at least, were attracted to architectural design and overall quality, not just to function. These had to be part of our story in this community.

Moreover, we determined that residents expected a "full-service" church, not just a place for weekly worship. They wanted a church that served all of their needs related to the meaning of life, not just their immediate personal needs regarding parenting, marriage, and the like. The community tended to think about relating to God as part of life with business partners, family members, neighbors, and eventually brothers and sisters in Christ. These educated, socially involved suburbanites naturally understood religion as dynamic relationships—which was partly why they desired to affiliate with a "quality" church that would "speak" to the community.

Maintaining a Public Presence

Without a building, however, we had to show that we were seriously committed to high-quality, meaningful, unembarrassing worship. We rented a 1,100-seat theater for our first-anniversary Easter celebration. This alone spoke loudly to our community as well as to those who had been meeting with us in homes for small Bible studies and classes. We recruited a fifty-voice choir, borrowed an organ from a dealer in a nearby shopping mall, and advertised aggressively. Over 750 persons worshiped under the auspices of our year-old church, which had no building or even a building fund but was educating residents in homes, had contributed thousands of dollars to benevolence and missions, and had a thriving youth program led by a well-respected professional sports personality.

The Easter service generated several invitations for me to participate in community and business meetings by offering prayer and frequently a speech. It also confirmed our belief that the

Spirit was already in our community, doing remarkable things among all generations. Our outreach increasingly seemed like it was primarily a matter of being faithful within the Spirit-initiated movements already underway. Other public activities similarly helped to build our reputation as a serving congregation. Our women's Bible study class began donating books annually for the religious section of the village library. In order to make sure that the books would serve the public, our minister of education carefully composed the bibliography. He also held an annual seminar for public school teachers on subjects related to their profession in the light of current church-state regulations and appropriate Christian responses. This fostered an ongoing community dialogue with those who influenced the village's children but might not affirm the value of a biblical world-and-life view.

With the expertise of our minister of education, the church trustees established a preschool board that eventually planned and executed a high-quality program for the entire community, not solely or even primarily for the church itself. Our objective was to base the curriculum on the academic and behavioral expectations of the local public school kindergarten in order to prepare children for interpersonal as well as academic success in the classroom. We had learned that residents in our area generally wanted their children to have every possible educational advantage. So our preschool opened with outstanding staff and facilities, sending a clear message that we were there to serve well.

In order to pursue our goal of serving the broader community, we did not first announce the opening of preschool registration in our church bulletin but instead sent mailings to the broader community. This resulted in a class with only two students from the church. The parents of the children were required to meet with the teachers periodically and to assist their child with homework assignments, which were carefully graded by age and included biblical subjects. Many kindergarten parents and their children became involved in our worship and children's ministries.

In our zeal to be public witnesses, we tried various forms of personal outreach that were not effective. For instance, I became a friend of a Christian who was a partner at a local hotel. We discussed the pros and cons of using the Lenten season to speak about our faith to the business persons and hotel guests who ate in his main dining room. For six Fridays during lunchtime, I spoke to a sizeable audience in his beautiful facility. Although it seemed like a good idea, the results were hardly worth the investment of time. In that setting, people wanted to eat and socialize, not hear from a local pastor!

By contrast, a physician and I had lunch in the same dining room and hatched a fairly humble, suburban-sensitive plan that bore considerable fruit. Since many friendships are formed around meals and conversation, we decided to try holding eight monthly meetings annually in a village location, serving a nice breakfast and giving attendees an opportunity to listen to known national leaders from a variety of professions and occupations. Our purpose, in addition to fostering fellowship among local leaders, was to strengthen ethical values in society by presenting exemplary leaders who could articulately address many of the moral issues of the day.

We recruited interested members of our church, formed a board of directors, found a volunteer executive secretary, and incorporated under a constitution as "The Executive Breakfast Club of Oak Brook." Since this was not a church organization per se, the church would not have to provide oversight or even be directly responsible for funding and administrating it. The church pastor would serve as the "chaplain" for the group, sitting on the lay board and opening the breakfast meetings with prayer. An unwritten rule was that the chaplain would select the Christmas speaker for the December meetings. For a fee, membership would be open to all residents who agreed with the club's purpose. This group would serve as a catalyst for ongoing dialogue about the deepest ethical issues of the day that faced many suburban professionals.

All of the above seemed to "just" happen. But nothing "just happens." Behind it all was the principal of planned spontaneity.

Other community-focused initiatives eventually included the following:

> Offering children's Bible schools and summer camps
>
> Participating in community functions, such as offering prayer at village board meetings and Memorial Day cemetery services
>
> Hosting Alcoholics Anonymous meetings
>
> Visiting patients and staff at the local hospital
>
> Providing a music conservatory, concert series, and men's singing group
>
> Teaching a literacy course for immigrants
>
> Conducting open houses for college students
>
> Serving as chaplains to the police and fire departments
>
> Founding an interdenominational clearing house and related services for the neighborhood homeless and poor
>
> Organizing a weekly men's breakfast with a devotional for church members and friends
>
> Sponsoring annually a regional conference on ministry
>
> Serving individuals with a small-group ministry for nonmembers as well as members
>
> Inviting the community each Advent to a live nativity

Each of these ministries has its own anecdotal history, but they all helped us to demonstrate our church story as both community service and gospel message. Some residents even voluntarily supported our church specifically because of our service to them in times of need. One father gave financially out of gratitude for the fact that I had visited his daughter while she was hospitalized several suburbs away due to an auto accident. At the time, she could not return home to care for her three children. I knew her as one of the residents who had attended my "Basic Christianity" course. She simply had no other source for spiritual support.

When a local woman was accidentally killed, my associate ministered to her family in grief. Although we did not know this unchurched family, the Holy Spirit brought the widower and his daughter into lasting fellowship with us. He attended services weekly and gave the church substantial annual gifts until he died.

We never served the community in hopes of eliciting such contributions; instead, we had been called to serve the village as good Samaritans regardless of other people's faith backgrounds. Nevertheless, major gifts arrived as we served, often totally out of the blue. They included customized coat racks for our foyer, blacktop for our parking lot, children's choir robes, a custom-designed chandelier for the foyer, an exterior canopy over the main church entrance, and 105 Shetland ponies. After spending three days studying about such fine animals, I reluctantly but gratefully asked the donor to give them to the governor of New Mexico instead of to the church!

Conclusion

Suburban ministry can be an incredible adventure in reaching out to residents. If there is only one formula for such ministry, we never discovered it. Instead we continued to be blessed by the unpredictable joy of service. After all, suburbs are filled with people who have spiritual as well as physical and emotional needs.

We discovered this truth early on, long before we had our own church building or any additional paid staff. Barbara and other needy residents taught us that by focusing honestly on serving the community we could demonstrate persuasively our commitments, values, and beliefs.

Discussion Questions

1. What are the "felt needs" of members of your community? How well are you addressing them? What opportunities exist to address them more effectively?
2. Where is the Spirit already active in your community or even within your church or church-planning group? How will you tap into that work of the Spirit?
3. What is your church's "story"? How and where are you telling that story?

Chapter Three

Suspending Immediate Judgments

I once hosted a local television program about faith. The format was a friendly but nevertheless adversarial debate between me and four current university students, only one of whom was a Christian. One student argued that true Christians could not live in upper-middle-class villages. He reasoned that genuine followers of Jesus would sell their excessive goods and give their money to the poor. He knew just enough about Jesus' teachings to be dangerously misleading.

Our spirited discussion led to the issue of whether or not a car was necessary. If so, was an automatic transmission essential? What about power windows? How large could the vehicle be before its size rendered it superfluous? Should white-wall tires and air-conditioning be acceptable for Christians?

Finally, the student admitted that if he were right then my suburban ministry would radically change. Every time a family joined the church—if they were willing to join such a church!—they would have to sell their house and most of their possessions and move away, where housing was cheaper. He sensed that this was wrong, but he had no alternative other than individual freedom. He was not able to distinguish between *having* and *loving* money, let alone between using affluence primarily for self or for others.

First Impressions

A lot of suburban churches fail because leaders implicitly convey a similar kind of disdain for middle- and especially upper-middle-class lifestyles. These leaders along with some members seem to see their role primarily as critics of those believers who are not as holy or self-sacrificial. Often without intending to do so, they instill guilt rather than gratitude, and dismissal instead of discernment. For us, the main issue was how to connect with suburbanites where they were in life, not according to where *we* wanted them to be in life.

For example, we wondered what would entice suburbanites even to try worshiping in a school gymnasium. Would they assume that we were merely a fly-by-night outfit? If they visited, what would entice them back for a second or third time? What would encourage them to bring along their family and friends? Clearly our good intentions would not be adequate. We had to win a hearing long enough to give the Holy Spirit an opportunity to awaken a deeper interest in their hearts. In short, we had to be Christ's love to them. We prayed hard and thought carefully about "courting" them. Our first impressions on them needed to be loving and caring.

We quickly discovered that motivation and expectation are mixed when it comes to attending church. Some suburbanites do visit a local church out of habit and expect the same kind of experience they had previously. Others come as family ritual; new to the community, such a family simply wants to do what it always has done on the morning of the first day of the week. Some have had bad worship or fellowship experiences and come begrudgingly, even hoping to leave disappointed so they later can tell friends, "I told you so." Some are dragged to church by a spouse who is praying for a spiritual miracle. Yet other visitors are new residents who are seriously looking for a spiritual home. Sometimes they have not been to church for months or years because their area church lost touch with the spiritual needs of its members. There are occasional visitors who have never attended a church and do not know what to expect; unless they are very extroverted, they are usually quite uncomfortable. In this latter group, a few are just curious, whereas more of them are passing through a dark valley and feel a need to commune with the Lord.

These and many other reasons move people to "try" a suburban church. We respected such varying motivations, hoping to meet the needs of as many visitors as possible. We had to, for we did not really know which of these types of needs would most likely motivate others to worship with us in a school gymnasium. Moreover, there was little we could do to dress up the outside of the building and the front grounds. What they would experience inside the building was going to have to serve us and them. In order to reach their hearts and minds during only an hour of worship, we sought to make worship so meaningful that they would eagerly anticipate the next opportunity to return—again and again.

We also realized the "givens" of our suburban area's potential visitors. They were middle- and upper-middle-class people who could afford the area housing. They were generally well educated. Residents were overwhelmingly families rather than couples or singles. Presumably they lived nearby even if they commuted to work via car or train. Surely they worked hard to get where they were in the social order. Since they were already able to claim the American dream, religion might seem more social and elective than urgently needed in their lives.

For these suburbanites, going to a gymnasium to worship had to seem odd, perhaps even undignified, unless they were curious or merely trying out a nearby option. Would they likely be willing to sacrifice time, talent, and money to help nurture the budding church, or would these busy people tend merely to come on Sundays and then disappear from congregational life? We especially worried about the latter possibility, given our temporary church home. We figured that we would not have a chance to build a Christian community in our suburban milieu unless these visitors could readily see that we were fashioning our ministry not only to win a hearing but to build a strong foundation for a long-term local church committed to serving its suburban village.

Suspending our judgments, we realized that we needed to make sure that we communicated the fact that we were there for *them*, not for ourselves. We planted this unostentatious church to relate the gospel to their existing ways of life, not to tell them how to live in tune with our own preconceived notions. With the essential insights of our founding families who lived there, I learned as the community outsider that the worst thing I could do would be to impose a way of life on this village. They taught me that our congregation was there not so much to critique suburban values and beliefs as to enable suburbanites to equip themselves with the power of the gospel to transform their own community as they would see fit. We agreed that we were there, in that unimpressive school setting, to learn how to serve these suburbanites within the parameters of their lifestyles.

Suburban Discernment

As pastor, I realized that I needed to help us be biblically wise and discerning even in our nonjudgmentalism. Otherwise we could slip into the kind of get-rich-quick "gospel" that has invaded some of the fastest-growing suburban congregations.

As recorded in John 12 and 13, a family of some means befriended Jesus. On this occasion, a dinner was being served in his honor. Mary, a member of the family, poured perfume, valued at one year's wages, over Jesus' feet. One of the disciples quickly objected, saying the perfume should have been sold and the money given to the poor. But Jesus, himself relatively poor, did not concur. In his divine view, it was not wrong to honor God extravagantly. Mary gave generously on the basis of her gratitude even though it is wrong to seek godliness as a means to gain riches (1 Tim. 6:5) or to love money and be eager for it (1 Tim. 6:10).

Moreover, Scripture makes clear that there have always been wealthy people in the church; some are good stewards of their abundance, and others are not. People's attitude toward wealth is critically important, for it will shape how they value and use it. Do they give sacrificially out of gratitude toward and love of God, or are they stingy and self-satisfied? In short, do they see their wealth ultimately as a gift for honoring God and serving one's neighbor, or as a measure of their own self-worth? This clearly is a great challenge for many suburban Christians.

We aimed to reach out nonjudgmentally in love in order to enfold residents in God's grace so that they, too, eventually could have the joy as well as responsibility to answer such questions as faithfully as possible. Only by ordering our messages in this way could we get a reasonable hearing that Jesus loves them and calls them to faithfulness. At this level, the message of salvation is universal: Whoever you are, wherever you are, regardless of how you have been living your life, Jesus died for you. In the suburbs, the ways that residents might feel the need for such love can sometimes be idiosyncratic. Often the message is that life can be spiritually empty in the midst of prosperity—that wealth itself is not an answer to the deepest desires of the human heart for love and peace. In other words, the "poor in spirit" can and frequently do dwell in the ritziest parts of suburbia. Still, accepting God's free gift of salvation is the place to begin. Ultimately this is the gospel message before it is the suburban message of hope.

But what about discernment—self-judgment for the sake of faithfulness? This next step in Christian suburban living is difficult. Accepting grace as a gift of God that has already been demonstrated on the cross should change how people live. Yet this cannot be a legalistic change, or a one-size-fits-all program where everyone gives away his or her wealth and moves to a less-affluent area—in spite of the fact that this can and does happen. Instead the message that needs to frame suburban worship and fellowship is what it means to give back to God out of gratitude, not out of duty or conformity. As I discuss more fully in a later chapter, guilt itself is not entirely bad; but overly ripe guilt, without adequate gratitude, can squelch a life of gratitude.

The other problem is churches that grow by turning the good news of the gospel into pop psychology. Today this is commonplace in rapidly growing suburban churches that replace heartfelt gratitude to God with a kind of individual or family happiness.

Their message seems to be that no one has to suffer—even that suffering and hardship are inherently wrong. One form of this nonsense appears as the health-and-wealth gospel of success—that with enough faith anyone can "make it" to complete financial freedom and even to extravagant wealth. Another form is the idea that affluence is necessarily God's will for everyone, so it should be pursued as a major goal in life. Supposedly once you get rich you then can think about giving back to God, as if God created human work and worship so that people could become self-righteously prosperous. Instead Scripture defines faithfulness as a kind of "living sacrifice" in which all believers give out of that which God has given them—talents and spiritual gifts as well as material resources.

For us as suburban church leaders, these were exciting questions and dilemmas that we wanted to address with the community, not without those residents for whom the issues were most relevant. We agreed that rather than assuming that we had all of the right answers, we would be faithful to our community by learning from the area Christians. Hopefully they might learn from us, too. We would grow with our neighbors, learning together what it meant to be faithful suburbanites. In short, we would together seek to be more like Mary. Our task at Christ Church was to cultivate a fertile community environment for suburbanites to make lasting spiritual decisions to follow Jesus, wherever such discipleship led.

Beyond Church-Growth Fads

In other words, our attitude toward the community needed to be respectful rather than coercive, disingenuous, or spiritually undiscerning. *How* we communicated with suburbanites was just as important as *why* we sought to serve them. So we became quite skeptical of church-growth strategies based on supposedly neutral techniques. Church growth is not primarily about tactics or techniques, however faddish. Occasionally they seem to work, but usually not in the long run. The fact is that lasting, faithful churches grow organically out of the sincere desires and shared dilemmas of the members and visitors. The problem of how to live faithfully in suburban culture is the very basis for honest, biblical conversations about what it means to be a suburban church as opposed to some other type of congregation.

A congregation has to figure out how to grow where planted. More accurately, the people themselves have to use the quandary of growth as an opportunity to learn to be faithful where they have been called and rooted. If the members and visitors do not take this journey together, there is little likelihood of sustained, deep growth. This is why asking the tough questions about ministry *in* and *for* and *by* the middle- and upper-middle-class residents of our area was such a blessing in disguise.

From then forward, we viewed our confusing suburban tasks, small and large ones alike, as important and God-given. We treated every predicament as an opening for greater wisdom and discernment, and vowed to let God do the impossible, as Jesus promised (Matt. 19:26). Our church-planting risks, including meeting in a school gymnasium, could be fertile ground for learning and living together, depending on how we approached them. We believed that inviting other residents into worship that expressed gratitude to God, and preaching about the tough questions of suburban discernment, would interest area citizens. We just needed to demonstrate to others that we ourselves were filled with the joy of salvation and were courageous enough to address these cultural issues without giving simplistic answers that our educated community would see right through. Our confidence needed to be not in ourselves but in the Lord, who would lead us as we appealed to him in humility and delight.

This kind of Spirit-led, entrepreneurial approach to reasonable risk-taking probably matches many suburban cultures. It is organic, resonating with the kinds of successful, goal-oriented, risk-taking people who live there. Many of our early members enjoyed the challenges of church planting and church growing, but they were also "market savvy." They kept us from making foolish decisions where we might have been inclined to naïvely trust God and not use our God-given gifts of reason and planning. We listened to comments from visitors about music, sermons, and liturgy. We learned by empathizing and reevaluating.

Was this a form of market research? I suppose so, but we never thought of it as a crutch, only as one more means of being culturally sensitive to where we were planted. Some church experts have said that this kind of cultural sensitivity is a means of being *seeker oriented*, but for us it was instead a way of being *finder oriented*.

How could we attract new members for a finder-oriented community of faith that would gather to hear the Word of God and leave spiritually renewed, enthusiastic about their faith, thankful for the Book that can so unfailingly guide Jesus' disciples today, eager to tell the world about their blessings, and secure in the context of the gift of eternal life in the kingdom of God? We could do this only by listening to God for wisdom and to those we aimed to serve for a deeper understanding of how to form a church body within their cultural context.

We remained open and creative, limited by biblical rather than cultural constraints. We continued listening to members of the village. We talked to merchants who interacted daily with residents, with the professionals who helped them stay healthy, with teachers who taught them and their children, and with civil servants who served them. We observed them in their yards, parks, clubs, and cars. We learned about their vacations, commuter and travel schedules, and sports events. We asked about the local schools, parent-teacher programs, discipline in family and community life, time usage, volunteers, and environmental priorities.

We did not pretend to be dispassionate, scientific observers; instead we opened our hearts as well as our minds to what we heard and observed in the normal courses of our daily interactions. We empathized rather than judged. The better we knew our "neighbors," the more likely we could serve them authentically without resorting to manipulative techniques or faddish programs.

Elements of Suburban Culture

Eventually we concluded that our suburbanites tended to have in common particular characteristics:

1. *Suburbanites are motivated from within.* They have initiative and dare to take risks. They launch new programs. They think independently. They have learned to assess and evaluate, to coordinate and synthesize, and to see relationships and interrelatedness. Therefore, the gospel must be presented to them with respect and in a logical and understandable way that is consistent with a larger, informed, and reasonable theological context. Peer pressure and other forms of external persuasion are not effective with such self-motivated, independent thinkers. Also, simplistic judgments will not get a serious hearing. Guilt, fear, and sensationalism will not usually motivate them even if they feel a bit of such emotions. They are too independent to be threatened, too self-satisfied and perceptive to be regimented. For good or for ill, they have come to trust their own seemingly rational judgments about life. For them, deep commitments come through vision, principles, and logical goals presented with compelling, consistent integrity.

2. *Suburbanites demand dependability.* They keep the commitments they make, and they expect others to do so as well. They do not intentionally make promises that they will not or cannot deliver. More often than not, they see through those people and institutions that do so. They have learned that when they commit themselves to a project or to people, they must be responsible. This tends to make them highly realistic people who will get behind practical projects with realistic outcomes but who will reject hyped rhetoric. This is also why they expect others to be reliable; they assume that others, too, have evaluated the realistic possibilities before committing themselves to a project or relationship. They will not tolerate excuses since they expect others to foresee the pitfalls and problems. They will not accept false promises or cute and clever gimmicks.

3. *Suburbanites practice specialized ways of thinking tied to a reverence for experts and authorities who really know what they are talking*

about. They admire people who have focused on a narrow area of expertise and gained a degree of excellence. So they also are inclined to employ and associate with people who have achieved it. In the education of their children, their health care, or their entertainment, as well as in the nonprofit organizations they support and serve, they expect polished professionalism and generally will not want to associate their names with mediocre methods or questionable outcomes. When they need answers, they seek out a top-notch professional and readily respond to the latest and best practices. For instance, they would not think of participating in a sport without the proper clothing and equipment and without excellent instruction.

In their view, the church must offer ministerial expertise. A church should be *the* place to go for spiritual and moral matters. They want to be sure that the church leadership has read the literature, is skilled, and has a network of reference with other religious experts. For them to trust a church and its leadership, they need to determine first-hand that the organization merits such deference. This puts a heavy weight on those responsible for the church's music, youth ministry, counseling, preaching, and all other church activities. Looked at through their eyes, the church is another institution that needs to be constantly updating its procedures and programs or it will not serve its members as well as it should.

4. *Suburbanites are goal oriented.* They thrive on action, but not for action's sake. They realistically chart the future and then hold people accountable for living up to that future. They cannot imagine any person, group, or institution not setting goals and holding itself responsible for meeting them. They demand deadlines and objectives, which they will carefully monitor. In their minds, an annual budget had better include objectives that specify not only how money will be used but how the use of those funds will later be evaluated. They are excited by documented progress toward goals. If a church, for instance, stops setting and striving toward specific goals, these suburbanites will move on to other goals, if not to a different, more proactive congregation.

For example, a woman in her late fifties or early sixties said to me, "My husband is in California half the time. He is buying another business. I just thought we were settled here in Chicago, but he cannot leave well enough alone." She wanted her husband to be successful. She herself valued organizational progress and personal growth. But she was holding on to other, more relational goals as well, such as the quality of family life. I regularly witnessed suburban households caught in spouses' or even children's conflicting goals. But rarely did I discover one whose members were all indifferent to progress of one type or another.

Along the way, however, the church leadership needs to attend gently to the conflicts sometimes caused by type-A, goal-driven persons. These include likely conflicts between some members and staff over how best to do ministry. More frequently, goal-oriented fathers and mothers tend to place high expectations on their children and can become overly critical when their offspring seem to underperform. Therefore, suburban pastors, elders, and counselors need to know how to address this issue compassionately with parents so their children are not antagonized in matters of faith as well as in schooling, work, and the like.

5. *Suburbanites are committed to excellence.* They give their best and expect others to reciprocate. They are not willing to accept a second-rate "product" in a second-rate context. If something is worth doing, it is worth doing well. If it is not worth doing well, it will not demand their attention or energies. So when they get behind persons and organizations that they know are similarly committed to excellence, they will not withhold their enthusiasm and support. Yet they reasonably recognize that excellence usually takes time and money, which they will gladly give as they can. When their own such resources are inadequate, they will recruit other, equally committed supporters.

6. *Suburbanites are confidently enthusiastic about the future.* Successful people are convinced of their abilities and impact. When they support a person or institution, they can be among the most enthusiastic and persuasive advocates. Their excitement is contagious, marshalling additional resources to the cause and often generating publicity through word of mouth. They are quick to

tell others about their latest projects and accomplishments, not so much out of pride as excitement.

In a secular sense, they are born "evangelists" for projects that can make a difference in the world as well as in church—and they expect others to be as well. The preacher, the Bible teacher, the youth director, and the choir master must be genuinely enthusiastic. The same goes for ushers and missionaries. Feigned enthusiasm is deadly, however, because these suburbanites do not have time or respect for it—and they can quickly spot such disingenuousness. Wannabe leaders who cannot inspire or who send negative vibrations will not survive in many suburban churches.

7. *These gifted achievers tend to have significant family problems and frustrations.* Broken marriages, chemical abuse, child abuse, poor communication, and little time for togetherness are but a few of the causes of suburban marital and family problems. As indicated earlier, their children often suffer from unbearable pressure to live up to parental expectations or reputation. No amount of status, popularity, country-club memberships, or money can solve these problems. Many of the suburbanites who seek pastoral advice, whether they are church members or not, live with major stresses and strains. Often the middle-age suburban women who suddenly show up at church are the first in their families to reach out for help in these situations.

Worship for Suburbanites

Given these characteristics of our suburban community, we sought to approach ministry in ways that would demonstrate our sensitivity to their culture as well as the church's biblical discernment. Most important was how we would approach weekly worship, which became the primary way that residents would check us out and, we hoped, find God in our midst. We aimed to be a community that nurtured such finders in the midst of their affluence and its related problems and opportunities. We never thought of using Sunday worship itself as a less overtly religious ceremony to attract visitors.

We aimed instead to grow the people that God sent to us by being openly and obviously a church with "traditional" worship— that is, apostolic worship with a Presbyterian or Lutheran flavor. This was our base for weekly worship, altered only in the sense that we wanted the experience of worship to be meaningful, rich, and vibrant. For us, this required excellence in the way we executed worship, not just humble gratitude for the attitude we brought to worship.

Our liturgy—the order and content of worship services, from greeting to benediction—had to be carefully planned for our particular village. We assumed that in spite of the residents' entrepreneurial spirit, they would want a more predictable yet well-executed service rather than one that struck them as faddish or contrived. Respecting the historic worship order, we included the following:

A call of God to worship
A grateful response by congregational singing
A cleansing service of humble confessions
A joyful celebration of forgiveness
Expressions of gratitude and love for God through music
    and offerings
A reading of Scripture
A sermon based on the reading
A sacrament as appropriate
A benediction with a blessing

We never thought of this liturgical flow as overly traditional and certainly not as mere ritual. For the sake of our planning, this liturgy accomplished three things. First, it connected visitors and members to the historic Christian church, including Christian worship's roots in the Old Testament tabernacle and temple communication between God and His people.

Second, it connected our suburbanites with most of the Christian traditions that they knew from their own childhoods or from other churches they had left. In other words, our worship did not strike them as irreverent, inaccessible, or lacking an educated understanding of church history. Regardless of which Christian tradition they were familiar with, whether Protestant or Roman Catholic, they would feel more or less at home.

Third, this order of worship gave us a rich, predictable structure for planning. Knowing what we had to prepare, we could focus on excellent execution rather than basic preparation. Everyone who contributed to the services knew what was expected of them well in advance. They could concentrate on creative ideas within their clearly defined part of the greater whole.

In spite of the importance of each liturgical element, however, music would most likely define us to visitors and the community. Music is the most "performed" part of worship; instrumentalists, vocalists, and directors are needed. More than that, they need to be as transparent as possible in order to draw congregational attention to the meaning of the music within the liturgy rather than to themselves. Music in worship is meant to communicate, not to entertain; to focus on the message, not the musician. This is why congregational applause can become so problematic as a response to music in the church.

Instruments and human voices join to express joy and gratitude, appropriately reaching congregants' souls and calling forth expressions of faith, love, and hope. Exactly how music does this is a mystery, beyond purely rational analysis. Still, gifted musicians learn by instinct and experience to discern what will serve worship well. In a sense, they partner with God to capture human hearts, which join together in collective praise, contemplation, and commitment to their Creator and Redeemer.

We also assumed that all of our careful planning and execution would not nurture open, God-directed hearts unless we conducted the music and the rest of the service with sincere hearts, in spirit as well as truth. In other words, we had to give our imperfect but most sincere, God-directed best in the planning and especially the doing of worship. This is why in the Hebrew and Christian traditions excellent worship must be fitting for *God*, not just for the *people*. Above all else, worship is a sincere looking up to God. The idea that suburbanites generally want something less was untrue for our community. Without necessarily being arrogant, our suburbanites preferred excellence regardless of the worship style. And they viewed insincerity as incompatible with excellence.

Our worship, then, needed to provide the cadence for suburban participants' ongoing life journey into God-honoring service. Life in the suburbs has just as many ups and downs as other people's journeys, even if they are different kinds of starts and stops. Worship can help a new community of young and old believers express together and before God their hopes and fears. It can also help the congregation listen to their God week after week so that they become more obedient followers of Jesus Christ.

But what about the gymnasium? Could we make it feel like a space dedicated to hearing the gospel proclaimed and worshiping God in the midst of a relatively success-oriented village? We tried to accomplish this with a lectern draped with an emblematic scarf, with padded folding chairs, with fresh flowers on appropriate stands, and with hymn books with golden embossed lettering on the covers. A greeter at the door and ushers in the aisles distributed specially designed bulletins containing our liturgy for worship and announcements for the week. In adjacent kindergarten rooms, a clean nursery was available for preschool children.

As preacher, I wore a robe appropriate to my ministerial office. The soloist and accompanist were at least semiprofessionals who could convincingly lead the congregational singing of well-known hymns. We tried to achieve a comfortable, relaxed, and hospitable atmosphere by avoiding stuffiness in our countenances and words. We offered our service and suggested opportunities for visitors to serve, learn, and give of their talents. There was no pressure or obligation, no solicitation or even mention of money. We quietly took an offering without any accompanying appeal for funds; no one could tell if someone placed a dollar or a large check in the offering plates. We pursued excellence sincerely, without airs.

Conclusion

When I got into the spirited but friendly TV debate with the university student, I tried to show that all real cultural engagement requires believers and nonbelievers alike to suspend any immediate judgments. I also hoped to demonstrate that biblical discernment includes how we communicate with those outside the church, not just our biblical insights into the good and bad aspects of particular cultures.

Suburbanites can be hard-nosed at times, frustratingly over-demanding and opinionated. But they do represent many of society's leaders, who have the power and authority to change things for the better. Some churches are called to love them by ministering in their midst. Such churches have to study their ways of life and pray for an understanding of their spiritual needs and dilemmas. They especially need to offer a vibrant, authentic worship, even in a school gymnasium. In short, they must learn to relate the gospel to their culture, without gimmicky programs or pop psychology. They must become faithful risk takers who suspend immediate judgments for the sake of lasting spiritual relevance to the community being served.

Discussion Questions

1. What kinds of stereotypes do you and your new, or established, congregation hold about your area residents? How will you assess their accuracy?
2. What motivates residents in your community to "try" a church? How have you addressed those motivations in the ways you reach out to the unchurched?
3. Which of the suburban characteristics listed in this chapter seem to apply to your community? How will you address relevant characteristics in your worship venue and services?

Chapter Four

Energizing Volunteers

A few congregants asked me about forming a men's breakfast group. They offered to prepare the meal if I would speak at their 6:30 a.m. meetings every Thursday. Being a night owl, I hesitated. Their rise-and-work business attitude was hardly my style.

On the one hand, a weekly men's breakfast was a terrific idea. Their motive was laudable: they sought to invite the community as a sign of church hospitality. On the other hand, I already was conducting semimonthly adult Bible studies and another class on Thursday mornings. Moreover, the bulletin material was due every Thursday morning. The men's breakfast message would take hours of preparation on Wednesdays in order to meet the standards I had set for myself. Yet how could I refuse these ambitious men who were themselves busy with other volunteer activities in and out of the church?

I finally realized that I didn't really have a choice. The best I could do to protect my time would be to become the sacrificial volunteer in their eyes, bowing out occasionally by pleading my own excessive busyness. But that rather selfish attitude could then infect the entire congregation. I thought to myself that ministers must always be the kind of servant leaders they hope to form among congregants. Pastors ought not to sacrifice to the point of self-destruction but certainly to the point of becoming an obvious living sacrifice. So I prayed for courage and accepted the challenge.

Spirited Members

Almost as if God were sending me a clearly timed message, the men's breakfast quickly became a significant program in the life of the church. This seemingly simple program became one of the most important contributions to the fabric of the church's congregational life. It helped us build a much more far-reaching volunteer program, since it gave us a chance to get to know, and be known by, many talented persons. It brought men into the wider life of the church during a time when many congregations were made up primarily of active women. The men's group also provided an extraecclesiastical, essentially organic means for older, wiser men to mentor younger ones.

Finally, the weekly tasks required to prepare, run, and clean up after the meetings gave many participants an opportunity to serve others without the financial or status incentives that normally accompany professional work. Wealthy attendees could serve the less wealthy ones—and vice versa. Older men could reach out to younger ones and to peers, next-door neighbors, and sometimes even business colleagues or competitors. I learned never to immediately dismiss the power of the Holy Spirit to instigate congregation-serving volunteerism.

Learning about Volunteerism

Suburban churches offer tremendous potential for volunteer participation even among busy members. Well-run, volunteer-dependent activities, both short- and long-term, are the breeding grounds for thoughtful, creative leadership. Much more than staff-run, top-down programs, they can identify and equip youth through senior members to become kingdom entrepreneurs. In fact, the biblical mandate to "subdue" the creation includes the entrepreneurial function of developing new ways of glorifying God by serving others.

Financial compensation is not always the only or best way of achieving creativity in the church. Volunteers can learn to put a servant motive ahead of self-interested benefit. In the suburbs, where so many residents are taught implicitly and explicitly to achieve greatness for the sake of personal gain, this Christian motive is especially important to model. Young people who see in their parents and grandparents the joy of church and volunteerism are much more likely to serve a congregation when they move into adulthood.

Sustained church growth inevitably depends on active, effective volunteers. Unfortunately, many seminaries fail to address this fact, acting as if pastors are the only leaders and should be left to their own devices. So many pastors end up either trying to do everything themselves or giving too much responsibility to volunteers without adequate training and organization. Both scenarios can mire a church in stress and conflict, leading to unmet promises, disappointed volunteers, scapegoating, and general disillusionment about the future of the church.

Yet pastors and lay leaders need to move ahead cautiously as well as enthusiastically with volunteers. I found it helpful to use these methods:

> Practicing trial and error
> Calling senior colleagues at other churches for practical as well as strategic advice
> Searching libraries and bookstores for materials written by other pastors and lay leaders
> Learning from successful lay leaders in business and nonprofit organizations who had joined the church

Some seminary professors can be helpful as well, especially if they have experience working with congregational volunteers. Although seminary faculty interest in preaching and worship has grown recently, practical volunteerism is still largely absent from published studies. The best sources are still management rather than ecclesiastical research. So I and other staff and lay leaders read a lot of management materials, always mindful of ideas that could be applied appropriately to the church.

Realistic Volunteerism

The problem is that volunteers' desire is insufficient; they also need to know *what* to do and *how* to do it. Moreover, they require a line of authority—someone to report to for problems and encouragement. Before proceeding, suburban church leaders need to ask some tough questions about every volunteer assignment and every volunteer:

> Is the work truly a priority at this time?
> How will this work directly support the vision of the congregation?
> Is the volunteer better suited for a different, more immediate task?
> Is a budget needed?
> Does the pastor support the person in this position?
> How can progress be evaluated?
> What is the schedule for completing the work—or for planning ongoing tasks?

We once mistakenly tried to shorten this process by not asking and answering the questions satisfactorily. Being relatively small, we assumed that the entire congregation knew that we had a building-fund loan that had to be supported, since the congregation had voted in favor of the loan to finance some early construction. Fund-raising to reduce the debt seemed to be in order, since we had to pay for what we had voted to do. We just assumed that suburban pockets would voluntarily offer the necessary funds.

Then we made an overly quick and comfortable appointment of a volunteer to plan and run the fund-raising. He quickly came to mind because of his apparent business acumen, not because we knew him well enough to be able to judge his suitability for the work. The church board rapidly approved this person because a number of members knew of his strong administrative record of leadership in a large, well-known company. Eager to serve and not wanting to disappoint us, he readily accepted the assignment and agreed to recommend a fund-raising program to us within months. Everything seemed to be going smoothly, particularly because all we really needed to do was remind members about our space needs, the purpose for the building expansion, and how much we needed to raise.

As it turned out, he was the right person at the wrong time. Rapidly advancing in his company until he was stretched far too thin, he was soon without a job and even planning to move out of the community. Perhaps embarrassed, he failed to ask us for help and had not made any progress on the drive. Since we lacked lines of authority, we were unaware of his predicament until it was far too late. The whole building-financing program was precariously close to falling apart, and we had no backup plan. We had thoughtlessly overlooked the fact that success-oriented, hard-working businesspersons rise and decline, change firms, seek greener pastures, and sometimes overcommit themselves to the point of failure. It would have been easy for church leaders to blame the volunteer, but those of us on the board were at fault.

We learned two important principles about working with our suburban leaders—and we found success in our subsequent fund drives and other volunteer management by closely adhering to them.

First, we made sure that volunteers knew up front the demands of the tasks. In this case, we wrongly assumed the volunteer realized the time-consuming dynamics of fund-raising, especially how to organize the congregation for a financial drive. We failed to recognize that he did not know our congregational giving habits and methods, our previous negative and positive experiences, and the resources available to him for this critically important task. To him, developing the plan for a church was a new kind of project that required some research on how to develop and run such a campaign for our specific congregation.

Second, we thereafter considered the immediate qualifications and personal situation with each potential volunteer. Since we failed to do our homework in this case, we owed an apology to the eager volunteer. We should have been sufficiently aware of his circumstances, offering him a confidential opportunity to share them with other church leaders, including me. We failed to serve him satisfactorily, so he understandably failed to serve the growing congregation.

The main concern in suburban church volunteerism, then, is congregational oversight. The success or failure of volunteer-led or volunteer-extensive efforts lies squarely at the feet of church leadership. In a newly planted church there might be only one person who is acquainted with every new member—the pastor, who has been instrumental in admitting them into the fellowship and best knows them. Still, the pastor needs to assess a volunteer's background, faith experience, knowledge of Scripture, and willingness to serve wholeheartedly in a specific area of service. The pastor normally has to make a judgment as to fitness, competence, and risk in every appointee. Although he or she can seek references to help make decisions, the pastor bears primary responsibility for any significant volunteer appointments. I learned over the years to get to know new members before asking them to accept such appointments.

Serving in Suburbia

Like Jesus' early followers, and in spite of their busyness, many suburban disciples today want to serve. They desire to be stirred by Jesus' call to put down their nets and follow him. New members, in particular, typically want a significant, tangible part in God's work. They desire to build the kind of community that will attract others with aching hearts, just as they were attracted to the church. Even though some of their enthusiasm can be unrealistic in the face of organizational realities, they want to be useful; to assume responsibility; and to feel trusted, appreciated, and respected. In short, a considerable number of suburbanites typically want to exercise their faith and stretch their spiritual muscles as long as they embrace the church and are committed to its vision.

But like Jesus' early disciples they can easily overcommit themselves. Their levels of spiritual maturity and ecclesiastic discernment are not always adequate for the volunteer tasks ahead. At work, they might have staff to carry out most of the everyday duties, whereas at church they probably have to do the work themselves. At the office they know the conflicts and challenges as well as the opportunities, whereas they might lack knowledge of, let alone insight into, the internal dynamics of the congregation. Eagerness and overcommitment go hand in hand when such gifted volunteers transfer their considerable lay skills to the developing congregation.

Lay Leadership

The potential for lay leadership among busy suburban members is enormous. When our church was about twenty years old, a congregational survey showed that 40 percent of the adult members were active volunteers. Why? Because these members wanted and even needed to participate in the life of the church as much as the church depended on their skills. We determined that recruiting volunteers is not as difficult as matching the spiritual maturity and giftedness of the volunteers to tasks worthy of their best efforts. These do not have to be tasks requiring professional abilities—as the men's breakfast volunteers proved. Nor do they have to be highly visible tasks that would bring notoriety to the volunteers. But they do have to fit the person's own abilities and desires at the time.

While it is tempting to place a notice in the bulletin or make an announcement from the pulpit that volunteers are needed, this kind of wide-open, want-ad approach is not appropriate when special lay gifts or skills are needed. The fact is that some of the more available suburban members will volunteer for practically anything; they often assume that the only requirement for any task is a heartfelt desire to serve. This is why the pastor and other emerging leaders need to get to know the membership if they truly want to leverage volunteer talents.

Volunteers for large tasks normally should be chosen from among those who have succeeded humbly in lesser tasks. Jesus said that those who are faithful in small things will be given larger responsibilities. Even if lay leaders have been successful in the past, they should be assessed carefully if they have asked for or sought credit for their previous work. If a job gets done well on behalf of the congregation, it should not matter who gets the credit.

In order to help a volunteer succeed, a church leader needs to explain the tasks in person, not merely over the phone, via letter or e-mail, or through a third party. Only after explaining the job and answering the potential volunteer's questions does it make sense to ask a busy suburbanite for a commitment. In the best of cases, the one to meet with the volunteer should be the one to whom the volunteer will be responsible.

No volunteer task should be treated casually, especially in the early stages of suburban church planting. Who can say that serving refreshments or ushering is insignificant to a visitor? Sometimes the slightest indifference or short attitude on the part of a volunteer gives visitors a foul impression of their entire church experience. Seemingly small things become big to visitors who are initially a bit uneasy.

Hospitality—making room for the stranger—demands that volunteers as well as staff treat visitors as if they were serving Christ. So it is a mistake to tell a potential volunteer, "This will not take much of your time," or "We will not burden you with a lot of work." Who wants to accept a task that the supervisor or even the pastor says is unimportant? Sometimes even the tiniest acts of kindness mean the most to visitors and new members.

Suburban churches tend to be mosaics of people with unique experiences and gifts. Members likely represent different nationalities, races, and traditions. Any serious church plant or revitalized congregation will wind up with an incredibly wide range of people from churched and unchurched backgrounds. Some of them will be skeptical of new ideas, and others will not have any church experience to use for comparison. For whatever reasons, some new members will not want to volunteer or even to participate actively in church programs. Others will try to become involved beyond what is good for their health and for the health of the church.

Dealing with Controlling Volunteers

Smaller churches are most likely to fall prey to aggressive people who have strong opinions and considerable determination to impose their will on others. Since small congregations also have limited human as well as financial resources, developing churches can too easily bow to the single-minded wishes of wealthy, forceful persons. Such individuals might offer to support programs to their liking or even threaten to withhold critically important contributions if they do not get their way. Often these are successful people who are understandably confident of their opinions. They volunteer aggressively in order to gain a position of knowledge and influence within the congregation. Critical areas for them typically include building programs, worship styles, and staffing decisions, including selecting and evaluating ministerial staff. If they do not get their way, however, they might be among the first to resign and switch churches.

Early in my ministry I accepted a call to a church that had such a member. Somewhat naively, I assumed that everyone knew I was called to be the primary leader, even though I would also be accountable to elders for the spiritual health of the congregation. When decisions were made at a congregational level, my word was final—or so I thought.

I soon determined that the influential member might someday withdraw his family's support, causing the potentially destitute congregation to shrivel up and die. This congregational fear paralyzed decision making. No one dared express any initiative that might provoke the ill will of the powerful family, especially the father. He was not a despicable person, but he was so self-confident and influential that he could single-handedly dictate the outcome of church discussions and the elders' decisions.

I had to break that controlling pattern if the church was going to grow as a spiritually mature, self-governing body of Christ open to all of the members' gifts. It would not be easy, particularly because the family saw me as a mere novice in ministry who needed their mature judgment. Of course, they were not completely wrong. It was my first church. They were just mistaken enough, however, to stifle my leadership. When church decisions needed to be made, the family was ready to speak up, and the father was anxious to volunteer his conditional support—conditional on doing things *his* way.

Soon after I arrived as pastor, I learned that the inside of the small wooden church building was being painted. The walls and ceiling were nicely decorated in tones of ivory and white. But the two, highly visible chancel doors had just been painted in the brightest orange imaginable!

I pulled aside the head painter and asked him to repaint the doors in dark brown. Initially he protested, fearful about crossing the influential church member who had also paid for the redecorating. But after I accepted responsibility, the painter covered the outlandish orange color with a fitting brown. In spite of his fear, I never heard a word about the doors from anyone, let alone the controlling church member. My simple challenge of ad hoc authority helped the controlling parishioner and the church to begin seeking collective rather than unilateral decisions. He later proved to be a loyal member of the congregation, and his volunteerism was a blessing rather than an obstacle.

Nevertheless, I was lucky that my impulsive actions had not led to major conflict with him and his family—and potentially the church. In an ill-conceived moment of my own possessiveness and young ego building, I had impetuously exerted my authority and violated a basic leadership principle. When addressing volunteers, church leaders should never high-handedly countermand the volunteer's orders without a fair and honest hearing. I should have asked the donor to meet me at the church, examined the doors with him, thanked him for his support, gently and respectfully made my case for a more appropriate color, and aimed for a shared outcome instead of my own heavy-handed reversal of his decision.

Facing Pastoral Pride

A church can function well only as a voluntary organization that cultivates and values the work of many members toward the common good. Early on in the life of the suburban church volunteerism must flourish, yet pastors can be major stumbling blocks because of their own prideful insecurity. They, too, want to succeed in order to demonstrate their value to others and to win the church's approval. For church-planting or church-turnaround pastors in suburban churches filled with professionals, humility is a fitting virtue for leading volunteers. Often a volunteer will know much more than a pastor does about the tasks at hand. As a novice pastor with little administrative experience, I discovered that many of my parishioners, especially experienced business leaders, could be of enormous value to our young church by coaching me. Would they be willing? Should I reach out to them? It was worth a try.

I therefore turned my vocational hat around and became the counselee instead of the counselor. I asked to meet in their offices, not mine. Before the first session, I found out enough about their occupation to ask at least one or two semi-intelligent questions (at least I thought they sounded sharp). This generally set the conversation in motion, demonstrating my interest in them and their expertise. All I had to do was make myself available to them to listen, observe, and learn, picking up skills and wisdom that were appropriate for church leadership as well.

Executives and managers can be difficult to reach, but my experience told me that they will respond quickly to their pastor. They delight in the opportunity to share thoughts, ideas, and experiences with the person they hear preach every Sunday. Most of them got to their positions of leadership partly by listening to others, learning about new things, and making wise decisions based on adequate knowledge. In spite of what some pastors think, these suburban leaders are not quick to dismiss a chance to learn from an interesting conversation partner. They will tell their pastor exactly what they think as long as the pastor is open and genuinely interested in their points of view. If a pastor respects them, they will respectfully tell the pastor how they feel about the church, the pastor, and the other leaders. When they invite the pastor to accompany them to events, the pastor has gained more than just a closer parishioner. The pastor has gained a friend, confidant, and sometimes even a long-term leadership mentor.

In one such friendship, I learned many lessons that have stayed with me. These lessons came naturally by way of example and casual conversation, not by formal instruction or didactic persuasion; I never felt "talked down to." Once I witnessed a young Christian business leader walk through the manufacturing plant he managed. Everyone he met treated him with warm, friendly respect, comfortably answering his questions about a sick child or a problem they faced. He knew them all (over one hundred) and their children by name.

It was obvious that this plant manager cared for them and that his employees in turn cared about him. It was no wonder that this young leader rose to high positions in both the business community and in civic and institutional affairs. He set for me a high standard regarding the way a pastor should treat church volunteers and staff. I think of him often as church leaders seek advice from me. My wisdom owes much to this man, who served as a kind of pastor to his factory flock. The way he worked with employees was how I needed to collaborate with church staff and volunteers.

Nonprofit leaders can similarly help the suburban pastor learn how to be a leader. At a critical time in the growth of Christ Church, the Boy Scouts' national administrator for volunteers joined our church. He eventually led our volunteer program for several years. I watched and listened as he applied his expertise to our growing list of volunteer tasks. While he reported to me administratively, he was more my teacher and mentor than underling. Those of us in the congregation who witnessed his efforts admired him and learned from his example.

In another case study in leadership, an experienced volunteer had already supervised the planning and building of major corporate campuses. He became the successful chairman of our church building committee for five major projects over a period of more than thirty years. Without his servant attitude and exceptional expertise, we probably would have made major mistakes. With his leadership, many elders, board members, and other leaders learned a tremendous amount about planning, building, using, and renovating spaces.

As time went by, we identified volunteers who knew more than our staff did about gardening, finances, kitchens, food, preschools, libraries, technology, utilities, and countless other specialized areas of service. While we followed and coordinated their efforts, they blessed us with their creativity and stewardship. All we did was identify their gifts, encourage them to volunteer, provide needed resources and training, hold them accountable in love, and genuinely thank them along the way. They assumed their places in our growing organization, respected and appreciated each other, and supported the vision and mission of the church in their work. As pastor, I saw my role as making sure that all of this volunteering would become a vibrant part of our ministry, not an end in itself that could detract from our mission to serve the broader community as well as the congregation.

Dos and Don'ts of Leading Volunteers

After thirty-two years as senior minister, I learned a number of things that do and do not work in managing volunteers. For example, try *not* to do any of the following:

> Play favorites—everyone wants to be and is important.
> Bend the rules arbitrarily.
> Accept mediocrity.
> Allow people to fail alone.

Expect volunteers automatically to see the larger picture.
Recruit someone who is marginally qualified in the hope that
    they will pick up the responsibilities well on their own.
Permit volunteers to move beyond their approved mandate.
Be afraid to discipline, but always with love.
Appoint a volunteer that you cannot discipline.
Ignore volunteers—any of them.
Expect the volunteer to create the need for the position of
    volunteer.

In contrast, here are things you should *always* try to do:

Support them publicly—even when you have to disagree pri-
    vately.
Schedule regular consultations.
Insist on excellence and integrity.
Be compassionate.
Express willingness to listen and learn.
Make fair and firm judgments.
Demand performance.
Use nonmembers only in secondary support positions.
Keep the congregation's story and purpose before them.
Match their experience to the congregation's needs.
Justify the need before recruiting.
Set regular terms rather than make lifelong appointments.
Recruit enough charismatic leaders to keep programs moving.

Conclusion

In every new and renewing suburban church, the choice of and
communication with volunteers is a major source of good or bad
congregational spirit. The pastor, in particular, inspires the right
level of mission-appropriate creativity and enthusiasm among the
volunteers.

If I had had this practical wisdom when the men's group
approached me about speaking weekly at their breakfast meetings,

I would have had a more positive attitude about their request. Stifling their efforts because of my own desire not to work so early in the morning on such a busy day would have sent entirely the wrong message to volunteers whom the Spirit was using and who are the lifeblood of our congregation.

Discussion Questions

1. What energizes volunteers in your congregation? What zaps their energy?
2. Who is responsible at your church for monitoring and assessing the quality of your volunteer efforts and volunteers? Who recruits volunteers?
3. Are there any persons or small groups whose controlling tendencies—however well-intentioned—interfere with others' desires to volunteer? If so, how would you address the issue?

Chapter Five

Assessing Preaching

I learned from my father a relevant concept for suburban ministry. The slogan on his hardware-store delivery truck read, "If it's hardware, we have it." He stocked three stories of items for erecting or repairing almost any kind of house or building. Tradesmen and the public came from all over the city, knowing that his store would probably have what they needed.

Suburbanites generally assess their church experience as if they are shopping for a spiritual "product" among numerous competitors. They seek a church that offers what they believe they need for their and their family's spiritual journey. This is especially true of how they view preaching and preachers. They expect, even demand "good" preaching.

"If it's preaching you want, we have it," I often said to myself. Excellent preaching became my ministry passion, my lifelong quest. Even as I witnessed the declining social status of ministers compared with other professionals, I never doubted the unique role that preaching plays in society, including the suburbs. No other profession in society is able to attract a weekly audience of people who want to be admonished as well as encouraged, humbled as well as strengthened. Yet no ministry tasks are more quickly praised and condemned. In fact, a minister's preaching tends to establish his or her value in the minds of suburban congregations.

Parish preaching is a highly personal activity. First, a pastor usually learns how to preach by consciously or unconsciously imitating other preachers, fashioning style and approach after them. Usually this just happens, similar to the ways that children become like their parents. Second, even in large congregations effective preachers speak as if only one person is listening—as if the sermon is meant for an individual rather than a "mass" of persons. Third, preaching connects believers with a personal God, namely, Jesus Christ. These three highly personal aspects of preaching are the beauty and the bane of contemporary biblical proclamation in suburban churches. The lay leaders as well as the pastor are responsible for ensuring excellent preaching, which they need to both understand and promote.

Communicating Creatively

The preacher's job is to figure out how to express a biblical text creatively, engagingly, and effectively to a particular community of faith. This is a miraculous and often mysterious process fraught with difficulties, since the preacher and the listeners are imperfect communicators corrupted by excessive ego, fear, disinterest, and especially in the suburbs, mental preoccupation caused by excessive responsibilities and chaotic schedules.

Without the creative potential of the Holy Spirit, preaching becomes a dismal art. With the Spirit, however, the preacher is able to (1) *discerningly* grasp the meaning of Scripture, (2) *reflexively* overcome at least some of his or her bad communicative habits, and (3) *empathetically* speak not just on behalf of God but also on behalf of listeners. These three Spirit-led, Spirit-opened, Spirit-developed abilities—discernment, reflexivity, and empathy—give preachers a unique power in church and community. When one or more is absent, however, suburban listeners tend to tune out sermons and shop for a different church.

Popular suburban preachers prove that preaching should be more like effective public oratory than a classroom lecture. They know that preaching should move people and not just teach them.

Augustine agreed with the great Roman orator Cicero, who said that public oratory should *inform*, *persuade*, and *delight* audiences. If it just teaches without persuading or delighting, a sermon is a mere lecture. If it just delights, the sermon is probably entertainment. If it only persuades, a sermon probably is rather shallow and manipulative. Although some pastors grow suburban churches quickly by focusing on pulpit histrionics, their preaching tends to attract primarily uninvolved attendees and members who are not committed to serving others as much as consuming for themselves.

As *communication*, then, preaching has to connect with listeners. Otherwise congregants are not likely to be moved to live self-sacrificial, all-encompassing lives of faith. When a minister stands before a congregation, he or she has to know how to address appropriately the lives of that particular suburban community—its members' fears, joys, doubts, hopes, anxieties, and the like. This requires creative study, planning, and delivery. It also requires suburban church leaders who will give the preacher helpful, honest feedback.

How Suburban Preaching Goes Wrong

In suburban contexts, preachers' creativity tends to go astray as they and their congregations mistakenly view pastors as *public therapists* or as *team coaches* that produce "products" for congregational "consumers." Preacher-therapists turn God's Word into bits and pieces of practical advice aimed at helping middle-class families patch up some of the cracks in their lives and feel better about themselves. Coaches use the Word too narrowly to persuade members and newcomers to get involved in church programs, as if preprogrammed busyness is itself a sign of spiritual life. In many cases, such enthusiastic coaches exacerbate the very problems of overcommitment and stressful busyness that already plague suburban overachievers who want quick material success more than patient spiritual growth.

Hybrid coach-therapists excitedly introduce one new church program—fasting, prayer, evangelism—after another, rarely taking the time to stop, listen, learn, and assess what has already occurred among members. Not surprisingly, the latest church-program fads, pumped by celebrity authors and promoted by publishing houses, usually enter the church scene through affluent suburban congregations that are looking for quick, prepackaged fixes for nearly any personal or spiritual problem.

Instead, the preacher has to grow in faith along with the congregation so that preaching becomes part of the shared spiritual journey of the church. To put it differently, the preacher has to live in a manner consistent with the truths that he or she presents. The preacher must be spiritually authentic in the pulpit, worthy of being listened to and followed. The congregation, in turn, must feel and know that the preacher really believes what he or she says. Sincerity has to be transparent.

This is critically important in suburban congregations today because so much suburban culture is predicated on image over substance. The suburbs are fashion-conscious, socially fluid communities where first and lasting impressions spring from job titles, cars, landscaping, and dress. Many suburbanites work in white-collar businesses that deal in words, logos, information, press releases, and other imaging tools. Increasingly younger adolescents size up their parents and pastors on the basis of style rather than substance. A suburban pastor typically buys into some of this facade making and eventually becomes tired of and cynical about it. She or he often feels the tension, wondering how to be faithful in preaching the Word to others who feel the tension as well.

This religious consumerism in suburban churches is self-defeating because preacher-therapists and preacher-coaches are themselves prevented from growing in spiritual wisdom and discernment. They become dependent on quasi-spiritual experts of one kind or another or even codependent with the congregation. Excessive busyness is a sign of ministers' arrogance and laziness—arrogance in the sense of believing that what the preacher is *doing* is itself of utmost importance, and laziness in the sense that preachers fail to make hard decisions about what is truly worth doing and what is likely to be a waste of time in the long run. The minister and the congregation have to protect each other from preaching that merely promotes short-lived enthusiasms that have little or nothing to do with communicating the living, often-challenging Word of God.

Preaching, then, is partly a matter of trust, believability, and authenticity—not just rhetorical skill. Why is it important for suburbanites to trust their pastor more than they trust local TV news reporters, stockbrokers, or department store clerks? Because donors want to be assured that their money will not be squandered. They want to know that the preacher lives out what he or she preaches, and manages personal affairs in tune with Christian faith. In short, congregants expect preachers to be stewards of *character* just as much as they are stewards of the church's material resources. Suburbanites are not inclined to follow a preacher who is constantly complaining and whining about the church or some of its members. When crises come, as they will, congregations desire to see their leader handling problems according to the precepts that he or she has preached—with kindness, gentleness, patience and other fruits of the Spirit.

By becoming part of the community in which he or she preaches, however, the pastor is vulnerable to the relational difficulties that plague humans. These include gossip, slander, broken promises, power plays, cliques, and verbal abuse. Suburban communities might appear clean, orderly, and even bucolic on the outside, but the underlying social relations can be deeply fractured, repressive, and superficial. Like their neighbors, suburban preachers can project a successful public face while being very lonely and unsatisfied within their own homes and even within their own souls. So they can be easily tempted to reach out to others in inappropriate ways, or at least to accept others' improper advances and confidences in hopes of being appreciated, affirmed, and trusted. Over time these improper associations can destroy self-esteem and require the preacher to knowingly put on a facade in front of the congregation.

Suburban congregants additionally expect their pastors to be well-experienced, well-read, culturally engaged preachers who know what they are talking about. Such a preacher has to be a nonstop learner who observes everyday life. Suburban preachers gain relevance by identifying sermon ideas, illustrations, and themes while walking, driving, listening to or viewing media, waiting in line at the store, and contemplating Scripture. A suburban pastor cannot reasonably hope to be a convincing preacher if he or she is not accumulating thoughts from congregants' daily experiences, electronic media, publications, and conversations.

Preaching Up

In addition, suburban preaching needs to aim high rather than low, thereby challenging relatively educated congregations to stretch their spiritual muscles beyond obvious exegetical and expository points. Most suburbanites dislike being preached "down to," as if a sermon should be pedantic or simplistic. Preachers have to be "simple but profound" without losing new believers and others who know little about historic church doctrine and theology.

The secret of congregation-building, suburban preaching is saying profound things in accessible, straightforward, relevant ways. Preachers who emphasize overly concrete, self-help solutions week after week create congregations that merely consume prefabricated laundry lists of spiritual "techniques." Members will not gain a rich appreciation of the faith, acquire a sense of their lifelong responsibilities under heaven, or grow in love of God and one another. They will not reach up for greater inspiration and wisdom. Nor will spiritually mature members spend time and energy waiting for others to grow. Instead many parishioners will transfer to other churches where the preaching seems to be meatier.

Spiritual Preaching for Head and Heart

Still, emotions generally play a major role in worship, specifically in preaching. Suburban congregations tend to want preaching that reaches the heart as well as the head. This is probably why some oratorically gifted preachers are able to attract megachurches filled with eager listeners who like entertaining sermons. The real issue is how to preach to suburban hearts while engaging suburban minds.

When I began to realize this heart-mind connection during my first suburban pastorate, I looked for ways of developing the part of my own life that was less theoretical and more experiential, particularly with respect to my biblical spirituality. I studied cognitive psychology and attended related lectures, looking for clues. I also began reading books on the developing topic of the human subconscious. At the same time, I prayed that whatever was underlying my own personality needs for a more heartfelt faith would become clearer to me. What was the nature of my—and presumably others'—desire for a deeper, more personal and more satisfying "relationship" with Jesus Christ? What might that relationship be like if it were both intellectual and emotional?

The ancient Christian mystics taught me that the church had always been led by those who not only knew Scripture well, but also fellowshiped closely with God. These great leaders sincerely practiced faith in the daily presence of God. My wife and I eventually decided to go to Spain and study the mysticism of Teresa of Avila and St. John of the Cross. At a summer session at the University of Salamanca, our journey led us to a life-changing discovery.

I sat at the feet of two spiritually rich persons—a Roman Catholic scholar interested in an ecumenical approach to the development of faith and a chaplain from Durham University in England who specialized in English mysticism. They represented a strange cohort for me, since I had been educated in Calvinism and taught to be skeptical about touchy-feely spiritual practices. Nevertheless, I witnessed my own eyes and ears—and heart and mind—being opened up to disciplines of the soul that over time led me to a new and deeper awareness of the presence of God. I began to understand the spiritual incompleteness that many Christians experience because of the neglect of the numinous aspects of faith. I learned that the so-called "mystical" dimensions of Christian faith are not irrational or purely emotional, but instead are part of the life of the Spirit that can deepen the more rational or doctrinal side of the faith.

When I returned from Spain, I and others began noticing changes in my ministry, including preaching. Congregants started remarking that something had happened to me as a person as well as a pastor. Many of them wanted to know more about my broader understanding of spirituality. But to this day I am not able to fully explain it. After Spain I still studied theology and attended to doctrinal insights. I continued preparing hard for weekly sermons. I continued reading widely and conversing candidly with congregants in order to be able to know and serve them well. Yet I was different, more attuned to the Spirit as I studied, preached, and worshiped.

I would never define this personal transformation as a second baptism or as my "real" conversion. Nor would I say that it must be every believer's experience, as if there is one road map for faith development. I share my experience in spiritual growth not in order to set myself up as a particularly holy or specially gifted person. Instead, I simply seek to remind church leaders that Christian faith is more than apologetics and systematic theology. It is also faith in a personal God who comforts, reveals, and directs.

Church leaders, especially preachers, need this kind of emotional or relational connection with God in order to most fully reflect the love of God to others in intangible but real ways. It is more than a mere human project, although it is accomplished *by* a person *for* persons, and *through* the inspiration of a personal God. As communicators, preachers should connect with the whole listener, not just the rational dimensions of congregant's being. The church has nearly always done this with music, including the singing of Scripture—which is probably one of the reasons why debates about worship music can become so emotionally charged. Church leaders should expect preaching that communicates in a lively, personally engaging, and spiritually animated fashion. My time in Spain apparently made me more grateful to

God and more compassionate toward my parishioners, thereby enhancing my desire to communicate more holistically to my congregation.

Every time I prepare a message, I ask myself how it will help the hearer and worshiper experience the presence of God as well as better grasp the relevance of biblical truth. "True" preaching ultimately comes from the Holy Spirit to the heart of the preacher; from there, it is nurtured for and expressed to others. Such preaching is not purely mechanical or technical, and cannot be contrived. Congregants understand this better than most preachers like to think. Parishoners expect integrity from their preacher as they listen to sermons week after week and year after year. Not all sermons will connect emotionally and intellectually. Nevertheless, the pastor and other church leaders need to commit wholeheartedly to this kind of holistic proclamation in suburban ministry.

Perhaps this commitment is especially important to keep in mind today in assessing suburban ministry. Many suburbanites work in professions that demand extensive analysis and rational problem solving. Frequently, too much emphasis on the bottom line strains interpersonal relationships. Suburban residents understandably feel deep emotional needs even if they are skeptical about excessively emotional preaching.

Spiritual Spontaneity

A personal preaching style, coupled with a heartfelt commitment to communicating Scripture well to a specific congregation, rightly leads to lively, creative proclamation. A pastor who is marked as a "three-point" preacher, a storyteller, or a doctrinal preacher can wind up fulfilling the congregation's stereotypes and make it more difficult for parishioners to listen carefully. The same is true for preachers who limit themselves to an expository, book-by-book, or text-by-text sermon series. Often without realizing it, preachers can become so tied to topical approaches or organizational styles that each new sermon begins to sound like previous ones even if the content is different. Attendees come to feel as though they can outline the sermon when they hear the Scripture reading. Such excessive predictability is not very stimulating, exciting, or comprehensive. It can squelch the spiritual connections among Word, preacher, and listener.

I always aimed to preach unpredictably—partly to keep my own interest in the creative process but, even more, to serve our suburban congregants, who appreciated new experiences and creative endeavors. Many of our suburbanites generally traveled to different cultures, read widely, and enjoyed considering novel ideas. They understood that truth can and should be expressed in various ways; for them, innovative presentations of age-old truth were nearly always better received. If I thought my outline was too predictable, I started over. If a parishioner could predict everything that I planned to say, then I did not have to say it. I had to either tell the listeners something fresh or confirm an expected message in a fresh way.

Hoping to avoid being stereotyped, I preached on biblical characters, parables, miracles, the teachings of Christ, topics, expository themes, historic doctrines, devotional points, comforting passages, motivating calls to service, and sacrifice. Our suburban members liked to read the biblical text and sermon title in the bulletin, and then say to themselves, "I wonder what he is going to say." They wanted to anticipate the unexpected.

Yet at the same time the congregation desired the predictability of pastoral identification with their lives. They wanted, and needed, to know that the minister understood their life challenges. They expected sermons that demonstrated the pastor's interest in what they were reading in the newspaper, seeing at the movies, or watching on television. They also wanted to know my biblically informed opinions, especially with regard to current social issues and faith-related controversies. If news reports were addressing the latest studies questioning Christ's divinity, they expected me to help them discern the truth. If divorce was overtaking their friends and neighbors, they hoped to understand how to build stronger marriages. Without offering simplistic answers but maintaining honesty and integrity, I had to be aware of *where* congregants were living, *how* they were living, and the crosscurrents of their particular experiences. This kind of identification with the congregation became the common "human" ground for spontaneity in my sermonic delivery.

Although my sermon organization emerged "spontaneously" from my interaction with the biblical text, on the one hand, and the "text" of contemporary suburban life, on the other, it always supported one main purpose. For each sermon, I would clarify whether I sought an intellectual, experiential, or motivating result. What would most effectively relate to *my* congregation? The question I still ask myself on behalf of the parishioners is "So what?" What difference should this upcoming sermon make in their lives? I wanted every person to leave our service saying two things in his or her heart, if not out loud: "I'm glad I'm a Christian" and "I love that Book."

Rather than relying too much on my own research and intellect, I learned to open my heart to the promptings of the Holy Spirit. I still begin by talking to the Lord about what he wants me to say and how he wants me to organize his material on behalf of his church. This kind of conversational prayer style has blessed me with many insights as well as eased my anxiety about communicating on behalf of God. Every pastor who has thought about it knows, as does every reflective congregant, that God can and does use purely human words spontaneously to accomplish more than the preacher ever intended. In other words, the Spirit takes the imperfect structure and content of a sermon and uses it to communicate more than what the preacher puts into it. The Spirit restructures and reexpresses it in the minds and hearts of listeners.

The power of the Spirit to speak through a sermon is incredibly important to remember because even suburban churches are remarkably heterogeneous in terms of personal experience, age, backgrounds, and interests. The preacher tries to connect with all of those disparate minds and hearts, but he or she will never get everyone mentally and emotionally involved in any biblical text or subject, no matter how expertly the message is organized and delivered.

Not surprisingly, some preachers grow frustrated. The typical preacher is never satisfied because he or she is always reaching for a better sermon that connects with more listeners. In most cases, the preacher knows the flaws, unless she or he never observes yawning parishioners or never seeks feedback from attendees. Yet every sermon has to be either discarded or delivered at some point. If the preacher waits for perfection, the sermon will never be offered to congregants. At some point the sermon must be locked up, finished. For me, that was always the previous Saturday evening.

Helping Your Preacher Serve You

Congregations can help their ministers preach well by conversing informally with them about their interests and lives—the things on their minds and in their hearts. Our suburbanites were interested in three things: people, events, and social movements (e.g., a celebrity, a news report, and a political or cultural trend and its underlying ideas). They found most interesting the sermons that addressed social movements, especially the concepts or deep-seated cultural assumptions behind social movements.

Why would suburbanites want to know why people, cultures, subcultures, and religions believe and do particular things? Probably due to their education, travel, and associations with successful people. They generally know what is happening in society, but they are uncertain why these things are occurring. Also, they work in profit and nonprofit arenas where social change is critically important to their profitability or other measure of effectiveness.

"Preaching up" was my way to make the faith relevant to those who shared their lives with me. I learned to live and work in the world of social movements and underlying ideas. For example, members were interested in the implications of new approaches to child rearing, managing, entertainment, and the arts—and how these trends compared with biblical understandings of human nature as well as the role of social institutions in society. By addressing social movements, a suburban preacher can usually gain both relevance and discernment among educated congregations without having to rely on gimmicky stories, tired jokes, and therapeutic solutions.

Conclusion

Years ago, a local preacher would have been the only public speaker that most people listened to from week to week. Today, with broadcasting and the Internet, laypersons have access to many fine speakers. Suburban pastors compete with these high-profile, celebrity-oriented, mass-mediated communicators who have all of the tools and staff of modern society. Preachers can try to compete head-on with polished media stars, or they can authentically serve their own parishioners without manipulation.

In suburban settings, where therapeutic preaching and religious coaching are increasingly common but poor substitutes for the real thing, the need for solid, congregation-serving preaching is critically important. Every suburban church ought to be able to hang a sign out front that says honestly, "If it's preaching you want, we have it." By working together, suburban church members can make this saying true for their preacher.

Discussion Questions

1. What does your congregation desire in preaching? What does it need? Why?
2. How creatively does your preacher proclaim the Word? Explain.
3. How can your church's lay leaders best help your preacher serve your congregation?

Chapter Six

Attracting and Caring for Staff

Due to church growth, our board authorized a search for an experienced associate pastor. We needed a caring minister with outstanding communication skills. Soon the staff and board interviewed our top candidate and agreed that he was the one to hire. Next, the candidate and his wife would spend a weekend with our congregational leaders, who would officially present the "letter of call" and finalize employment details.

At a leisurely Sunday brunch when we were to present the letter and establish a moving date for the pastor's family, the candidate's wife was visibly upset. She adamantly opposed the employment proposal, said that she did not want to move to the Midwest, and indicated that she was not interested in church activities. She fled from the table in tears. After a private discussion with the candidate, we all agreed that we should not proceed with the call. We seemed to have made a mistake.

This embarrassing situation resulted because of my failure as pastor. I soon apologized to the church leaders and to the candidate for not including the pastor's spouse earlier in the interviewing process. I learned that churches hire whole people, not just employees. These staff persons, in turn, generally are the "faces" of the suburban congregation. The staff's "countenance"—the quality of its work, its overall demeanor, its attitude toward serving others, and its commitment to the good of the congregation and the community—must be nurtured so that members relate to each other not just as professionals—which suburbanites are apt to do—but also as part of the family of Christ.

Learning from Mistakes and Masters

Staff relationships should include workers' families, not just the employees themselves. We regularly welcomed new employees' spouses and children to potlucks, where we tasted each other's dishes, shared kitchen chores, told family histories, offered unsolicited words of welcome and encouragement, sang together, and listened to our children's banter while discussing their talents. We also prayed personally for each other. When appropriate, we celebrated birthdays, anniversaries, marriages, and farewells. For us, staff appointments were vital for the health of the congregation, not just for the quality of our work. We never fully separated relationships and work, since each had to feed the other for the good of the employee and the entire congregation.

I learned such staff bonding at the feet of excellent managers and administrators. Living in our area, they constituted the church board to which I was accountable and with which I met monthly. I also arranged to have each ministerial colleague and department leader meet semiannually with one of the board members for personal counsel and advice, so we all could grow together.

I learned that people often move to the suburbs in hopes of securing a better, more enriching environment for themselves and their families. In our village, new residents justifiably looked forward to the area's fine schools, shopping, public sports events, and churches. I realized that as we grew we needed excellent staff to provide outstanding ministry in tune with such suburban expectations.

For example, we needed gifted worship musicians whose skills could meet suburban expectations. So when we began looking for our first music director, we contacted an excellent Christian college with a notable arts program, described our need to the head of the music department, and asked for names of the outstanding new graduates in organ and directing. He recommended, and we hired, a young couple—her as organist and him as choir director. They shared our suburban vision, trusted us, and became our first staff members.

Later we began looking for a person to lead our youth and educational programs. Requisites included a graduate degree in theology, ordination, a compatible world-and-life view, and a sense of calling to serve in our type of suburban ministry. Again, we discovered an exceptionally qualified person about to graduate from seminary. With his spouse's support, he enthusiastically accepted our call.

But I was naïve about the broader implications of this minister. Peter Druker once remarked, "I have never had a secretary. If you hire a secretary you will need a file clerk. Now you have an organization which demands your precious time." He was so insistent about this that he wrote his many books in longhand. If he was right, I was not just the pastor; I was becoming a personnel director for every minister added to our staff. I didn't want that. I doubt that most suburban pastors do. But what could I do about it?

Ready or not, I became responsible for the ministerial suborganization of our church. It was demanding, uncharted territory for me. Although the board took care of moving, salary, and housing for my new colleague, I needed to help him become productive, comfortable, and able to flourish amidst both failure and success. I could see myself enjoying preaching for decades. Like many suburban pastors, I could not imagine myself managing others. I began to realize what all suburban churches have to face: a conflict between most pastors' view of what it means to be a pastor, and suburban parishes' expectations that pastors should serve as excellent managers.

Since my new colleague's first ministry experiences were on my watch, I was responsible for his work. He depended on me to explain and advise. I was even responsible for his success in areas such as the youth ministry that did not involve me directly.

Some churches hire administrators or relegate staff overview to the board. I wanted to maintain responsibility for the ministry of the church, which meant that I was expanding my work to employee supervision. Nevertheless, we needed governance policies.

Deciding Who's in Charge

We concluded that the board should decide on policies for the governance of congregational programs and activities. I was responsible for *upholding* the policies, not for *creating* them. The board served the congregation by recommending nominees for the senior pastor and monitoring his or her work, but it was not in charge of day-to-day activities.

It made sense that the senior pastor would report to and be accountable to the board but not other staff or influential members, who reported to me. I had to bring staff nominees to the board for approval. I had to search for associates, assess their qualifications, and justify my choice to the board, which had the final authority to approve or reject. This organization established a clear line of accountability and spared the staff from multiple, conflicting authorities. It also gave the staff and me ownership in shared activities in pursuit of congregational goals.

Our talented board, composed largely of professionals, reviewed for approval every new job description, which included a new integration of descriptions for existing staff. Yet I learned this only after the board asked to see what I would be doing after I transferred some of my specific tasks to the perspective staff member. For instance, what were my responsibilities contrasted with those of the new associate pastor? By listening to and learning from the management-savvy board, I was gaining from their experience.

At the same time, a suburban board generally includes entrepreneurially minded members who recognize the need for a fair amount of ministerial autonomy. They want the pastor to serve as the chief executive officer, who is accountable to the board and who puts board-approved church policy into place. Suburbanites generally want a pastor who will keep the church on track through direct supervision or at least through other staff. This makes enormous sense as long as 1) the pastor is willing to learn how to supervise others well, and 2) the staff can and will assess the supervisory efforts of the pastor.

We accomplished the latter by pairing each staff member with a board member. These pairs met informally at least every six months, and staff members were encouraged to raise any concerns about my leadership so the board could address them with me. As a result, the board was better informed about the work of the staff as well as my leadership.

Specialized Needs and Church Specialists

Perhaps because denominations have not devoted adequate time and resources to most specialized ministries, churches increasingly depend on independent seminaries and parachurch organizations for staff hiring, training, and expertise. Moreover, some seminaries no longer educate their students in the ecclesiastical, theological, and doctrinal tradition associated with the seminary. This situation requires a church's extra effort for a more extensive doctrinal and compatibility interview of candidates.

Once in my haste, I abbreviated an interview process and took the candidate's word for his "generic" doctrinal position. When he joined our staff and began teaching and preaching, he dogmatically dismissed several controversies about major doctrinal subjects. His simplistic answers to theological quagmires, along with his lack of a well-articulated world-and-life view, became uncomfortably obvious. This problem taught us the importance of conducting a thorough interview on doctrinal compatibility even though we were an independent church. Suburban churches that deemphasize their denominational or at least doctrinal particularities in favor of a more generic "community" image have to face this issue if they hope to avoid future conflicts.

Some well-qualified suburban ministry specialists with parachurch or solo ministry experience find it difficult to transition to a ministry team. Often they have had the luxury of working for an organization that focused exclusively on their specialty, such as youth or singles ministry. Sometimes when they join a church they do not want to relinquish any control to colleagues who are not experts in their specialties. Also, they can be fairly ego oriented when they know that they have greater experience in one specialty, no matter how secondary that specialty is in the everyday work of the staff. They may even innocently seek attention for only part of a church's overall ministry, namely, the department that they work within. They are like golf professionals who want to be the hero of the game when they should imagine themselves as members of a team sport like basketball.

Moreover, church ministry is not an average job. It necessarily entails a deep spiritual commitment and exemplary behavior. It calls for integrity, honesty, and family-like loyalty in times of conflict. It demands virtue, even spiritual fruit: patience, forgiveness, and love for the unattractive and unlovable as well as the rich and powerful in a church. In our case, there had to be a sensitivity, and even empathy, for the type of people who live in the suburbs, such as stressed out, overworked, alcoholic, depressed, and driven persons. The staff had to respect them and love them as they are, not according to some humanly constructed ideal based on a hypercritical stance.

I once failed during an interview to probe the empathetic abilities of a potential youth minister. He was well qualified and soon won the hearts of our youth and their parents. As much as he tried to temper his critical feelings about suburban materialism, however, he found it impossible over time to be patient, sympathetic, and loving toward suburbanites who did not share his negative mind-set. Trying to force others to adopt his pet peeve week after week, he confused our youth and offended some parents. He became an antisuburban crusader who used his position within the church to criticize some members, policies, and decisions. Although gifted at youth ministry, he simply lacked the requisite spiritual generosity toward those who did not share his views. Since we had worked hard to be a suburban-friendly and even business-friendly congregation, this became a major stumbling block for us as well as for him. We eventually helped him relocate to the inner city, where his heart was and where he could more fully use some of his gifts without causing unnecessary division.

Ministerial "specialties," then, are not just areas of professional expertise but also matters of personal suitability and cultural fit. This is why an alcoholic is best helped by a reformed alcoholic. Often it takes one to know one, but even more so to empathize and love one. Someone who is patient and loving is more likely to win the right to be heard. Someone who "has been there" will gain a listening ear and evoke trust. A person who cannot identify with those who need to be served will not work out well in such ministry. It sometimes sounds trite, or at least overused, but the fact is that Jesus came down to earth and identified with fallen human beings even though he was God incarnate. He was humble, down-to-earth. By contrast, spiritual arrogance or self-righteousness tends to plague suburban ministry by destroying the staff's ability to identify with those in need. Suburban ministers, even at large, multiple-pastor churches, have to love those they serve.

In spite of my high hopes for some of my earliest recruits, I was disappointed. I worried about how others viewed me and the church as specialized staff. I tried to impose on new staff the capabilities and achievements I witnessed in "successful" churches. In my travels, I met church leaders who had exceptionally talented associates on their staff. I had a habit of picturing such staff as ideal for Christ Church. In my own interviews, I would try to impose on potential candidates a career track of my personal design. I had become arrogant, unable to identify with candidates based on who *they* were and what *they* offered.

Instead, I should have described each position as accurately as possible and then asked candidates what *they* brought to the team. What were *their own* strengths and experiences? I should have responded to each candidate's creativity rather than trying to rewrite each position according to my own borrowed dreams about specialized excellence. What was the value of making it easy for interviewees to agree with my ideas? I had failed to listen and identify with them. How could I possibly know what they could contribute to the church if my whole approach to hiring was trying to clone new employees?

I was a slow learner, but as time went by, I was blessed with some of the most creative, competent, and empathetic people in parish ministry. All they needed was the freedom to be creative. For instance, our minister of education, who introduced the use of computers in Sunday school, proposed that we could help other churches by offering them our expertise and software. After listening to his realistic dreams and heartfelt concern for ministries that were less computer-savvy, I agreed. Before long we hosted the first national computer conference for Christian education.

Remembering How to Serve

When I retired from full-time ministry, our staff included a core of experienced members who had served together for many years. As time went by, the more we shared about ourselves and our ministries during staff development meetings, the more we grew in mutual trust and admiration. By the time I left, the senior staff played a major role in our search and interview process. I, too, had learned to trust others.

Yet a couple of decades earlier I still carried a major part of the staffing responsibilities. So back then I periodically shared with the staff some of the wisdom we had learned earlier, hoping to help raise the next generation of leadership. When we reached 3,000 members during a major growth spurt, I nudged the staff toward an appreciation of our vision and our tribal story. Having been at Christ Church from the beginning, I told the staff at a retreat,

> The administration of the staff is sometimes misunderstood as a chain of command by which orders are handed down. In our situation there is no such thing. Our Board of Trustees was elected to exercise a position of authority for the congregation. . . .

This board makes it a point to know what is going on. I have discovered that their talents are available when they are informed and consulted. They are not in need of power but are mature enough to allow me and the staff to manage our affairs. When we run into difficulties, they confront me very critically, both positively and negatively. We are wise to learn from them and trust one another. In the eight years we have worked together I have benefited greatly and have never had reason to doubt their integrity. Please join me in gratitude for this great relationship.

One of my responsibilities is to make our relationships so helpful and supportive that the very thought of rump sessions to consider staff matters will not occur. Those meetings are the source of disunity and undermine the sense of fair and honest relationships. Please bring any misgivings to me. I am not the boss. I am here to help discover the most effective and balanced way to achieve our goals. I am the only person in the organization that is responsible for everything that happens and knows how the parts are all connected to the whole. I promise you my time and best effort to be of help. My door is always open. But it will not be of service unless you walk through it.

Once we have made a decision I will support it. I will never countermand your authority. None of us should ever negate or intrude on the territory of another staff member. If anyone approaches me regarding programs or activities regarding any of you, I will never make a negative remark or judgment. If I agree that a problem exists, I will talk directly to you. You should do the same for each other. If anyone tells you that I said something that you are to do or change, you can depend on the fact that it is not true. We must all play by the same rules and never pull rank. Always settle differences in private, not in public.

We must all have genuine and enthusiastic support of one another and our programs. I will attend as many functions of yours as I possibly can and is proper. Church members soon catch on to indifference and lose their enthusiasm. We all need loyalty to the church, to our purpose, and to one another.

Excellence is our objective. And when we fail, we will lean heavily on each other. This will happen, but not with permission or intent. It is part of the risk factor. It will keep us humble, teach us unforgettable lessons, and make us better servants in the future.

Let us thank God for our gifted friends and colleagues. Let us pledge to use the administrative relationships to build a better tomorrow. And let us rejoice that we share one of the unique opportunities to tell the greatest story ever told.

I repeated variations on that message for years. It was good for me to remind us, good for the staff to be reminded, and good for the congregation to experience the results. We all needed to recall who we were, whose we were, and how we would function together biblically, not just organizationally. We needed to keep alive our tribal story, or we would forget who we were as church staff. We were not merely suburban professionals, managers, or even employees. We were servants of Jesus Christ in a particular time and place.

Staff retreats were the opportune times to discuss such subjects leisurely, to share openly, to pray together, and to feed our spiritual as well as professional imaginations. At times we brought in others with special talents to challenge or enrich us. We played silly games, pulled pranks, and often gleefully embarrassed one another. We heard about our hobbies and adolescent mischief. We grew together. We were as diverse as the disciples of Jesus and just as determined to serve him. Often we failed, and forgave. Those delightful staff meetings represented a microcosm of the kingdom of God in loving action. They became days to remember. How did we create them so that they were worth remembering?

We held our regular staff meetings on Monday mornings. This helped us capture important reflections on Sunday's events, as well as on significant congregational responses to Lord's Day ministry. Staff leaders and their associates attended. Other staff, such as office employees, custodial staff, and administrative assistants, met instead in smaller groups with their supervisors. This gave the ministerial staff time to evaluate and develop the spiritual programs of the church. The agenda included devotions, reports by each staff member, announcements, long-range plans, and matters of staff interest.

Special occasions frequently included unexpected tomfoolery. When I turned sixty years old, church employees suddenly arrived with a cake, singing. I blew out the candles and opened my gifts, including a bright red cape, skullcap, and sparkling scepter resembling a cardinal's vestments. How dare they treat their own prelate so disrespectfully! The staff loved roasting the "old" leader. I cherished being one of the staff, not just the "priest."

We also discussed difficult behavioral issues at these private meetings. For instance, we openly addressed sexual misconduct, since ministry is well suited for temptation to indulge in illicit online and in-person activities. Ministry provides private encounters that stir the natural sex drives of counselors and other caregivers. Pastoral calls, in particular, can tempt the unguarded confidant into sexual intimacy. Yet who can be a real pastor without making such calls? And how is it possible to make them only when two ministers or a minister along with another church leader can make the visit together? We often lack the time or luxury for safeguards.

When I entered the ministry, I had no idea that I would be confronted with sexual issues in so many different circumstances. Frankly, I was naïve. I had no memories to call on because my own church background tended to sweep under the carpet any talk about sexuality, let alone any sexual issues arising in our denominational congregations. Sex talk was out of bounds except for a few discussions at my seminary.

In one class, a visiting pastor told us seminarians about the time he called on a woman who was at home recovering from an illness during a cold, winter afternoon. At his knock, she opened the door wearing a fur coat. She invited him in, took his coat, and sat in a chair facing him. They chatted for a few minutes when she suddenly told him what a wonderful pastor he was and how much she depended on his encouragement. Then she arose, quickly pranced over to him, threw off her fur, and sat down on his lap—stark naked! The minister telling this story hesitated, looked inquisitively at us naïve students, and waited for the obvious question: What happened next?

The pastor immediately pushed her off his lap, ran for the door, and dashed home. Then he realized that he had gotten so flustered that he had left his coat and hat with her. So he called his most trusted church elder, asked him to retrieve the coat, and pledged the elder to confidentiality.

That story is almost too Hollywood-like to seem real. But it woke us up to the need to be ready for the unexpected. Whether the unanticipated actions came from someone else or arose in our own hearts, we novice pastors would have to be ready to act wisely. We students agreed that we should do all that we could to avoid situations that could compromise our moral integrity. Because suburban ministry has become increasingly informal and relational, often for good, these kinds of concerns should be addressed openly by staff and by cross-congregational associations of ministers.

At our church staff meetings, we agreed that we often have too much confidence in our personal self-control. Ministers are human and therefore must not transgress the borders of temptation. So when my office in our church building was being designed, I insisted on having one wall open to public view, with sheer curtains that provided enough privacy to protect personal identity but allowed any actions to be clearly visible. My chair was in front of the window, which overlooked a garden chapel. It was a comfortable but safe setting for personal conversations, and it reduced my own temptations at the office. Presumably it deterred others as well. Even though I had a home study, I did not use that space for meetings that could even be perceived as inappropriate.

Staff Fellowship

In the suburbs, where people often are excessively busy, upwardly mobile, and goal oriented, personal relationships can suffer. This is particularly true among congregants who might not meet regularly with other members for fellowship. Friendliness among staff serves as a kind of congregational image of fellowship, a reminder to active suburbanites of the value of shared play.

As a fellowship-loving staff, we leaders allowed ourselves to become the laughing stock of the church family on behalf of the flock. One time the trustees asked the staff to surprise attendees with an unannounced topic and a staff-led performance during an upcoming congregational brunch. Previously the staff had planned such events together, sharing duties and agreeing on what needed to happen for an entertaining event. On this occasion, however, we met for our staff planning session and, unable to think collectively of anything new, assigned the task to our music director. He quietly discovered some latent musical talent and began to rehearse individual staff members. One person had not played the violin since high school; another, the trumpet; and another, the trombone. Yet another played the drums. For instrumental neophytes there was something new to try, perhaps a triangle or kazoo. One colleague even took up the keyboard just for the event. In time, the music director managed to get a marginally promising sound from each of us at a so-called "rehearsal." He gave me a baton and took his seat at the keyboard so I could direct this rag-tag group of semi-tuneful performers.

I had directed some pretty bad church choirs, but nothing like this. Nevertheless, we stumbled bravely ahead—or behind—by practicing together twice weekly. Finally, the day arrived, the first of four presentations before hundreds of people. We borrowed uniforms from the local high school marching band, taking on at least an appearance of professionalism. We had labored hard as well as had quite a bit of fun. But were we ready for prime time? I had my doubts. This could be a disaster, I thought to myself. We had to be campy, to play up our amateurism as if we were professionals.

At the great congregational event we solemnly walked into the room. When the band was assembled on stage, the name of our group was dramatically unfurled: "The Staff Infection." Then I entered impressively with a stove-pipe hat and director's uniform. We opened with "76 Trombones." A resounding disaster. Next came "When the Saints Go Marching In." The congregation clapped to the beat, probably to drown out the bad notes and help unify the players. The audience was invited to stand and sing along on one verse as an encore, after a brief introduction by the "band." Because everyone was having such a good time, I did this without the knowledge of the band. So they did their thing, too. I, with a great flourish, let fly with a dramatic downbeat. No one played! I almost broke my arm. A resounding success. All show and no content.

Such self-effacing staff relationships and activities helped us to understand, trust, sympathize with, and love one another. They made the more serious ministry much more relational and acceptable. They helped cleanse our motives and make mutual, positive criticism possible. They even opened the door for other, more serious conversations when we planned and prayed together. Finally, they encouraged the wider congregation to enjoy play and seek fellowship.

Renewing Work

One suburban church legacy will likely be a greater emphasis on for-profit management, including the idea of employee review. Given their location and makeup, many suburban churches have adopted board-initiated processes for evaluating and sometimes even compensating staff. We settled on a helpful system in which every staff member had to be reviewed by the person to whom he or she reported. As senior pastor, I was reviewed by a board committee. We came to these meetings with our own self-evaluation based on the goals and objectives agreed on at the previous annual review. If needed, evaluations were scheduled more frequently. These were productive, staff-serving exercises conducted with integrity. They established benchmarks for accountability and achievement.

These reviews taught staff to serve one another as well as the church. They made instructors and motivators out of those of us who conducted reviews, for we had been reviewed ourselves. Also, by recalling together our personal and institutional goals during the reviews, we were all better focused and had clearer priorities, opening the way for improvement within the bounds of the church's vision, not just our personal imaginations.

Unlike some churches, which fail to address staff weaknesses, we had to face our failures and admit them freely to colleagues. Similarly, we became justly skeptical of our own personal over-enthusiasm regarding highly touted external programs. Holding each other accountable, we were less likely to fall prey to the latest fads.

When we were searching for a needed men's group program, I read a glowing report about the activities at a large church near Washington D.C. With great anticipation, a layperson and I took two days out of our work week, flew to the nearest airport, and arrived at the church in time supposedly to meet with church leaders. A substitute for the men's group leader arrived late and was apparently unaware of the article I had read about the program. Eventually three program developers and leaders arrived, only to inform us that the program was still being organized. The inspiring article was a deceptive projection of a theory that was not yet proven. I quickly lost some of my excitement for undocumented claims about "new" and "highly effective" church programs.

Too often, an entire church staff gets pulled into such boondoggles because no one checks them out carefully. Our mutual accountability led us to review new initiatives before adopting them.

Unfortunately, church leaders frequently present inflated program data—as if hyperbole is a Christian virtue. Staff members are similarly tempted to use numbers to establish funding needs or to brag to colleagues about their "successful" ministries. Senior pastors are tempted to release hyperbolic data to compete with their peers or support growth claims. The larger the congregation, the easier and thus more tempting is this deception.

I encourage church leaders to visit periodically the various activities of each of their own congregation's programs, charting their personal observations for comparative evaluations. The easiest way to deal with a staff member's or volunteer's temptation to tamper with numbers is to remove temptation by randomly using sign-up attendance sheets. This policy inoffensively protects staff from any doubt about accuracy, and it is a valuable procedure for annual reviews, budget planning, and long-range projections.

Compensation Matters

Multistaff suburban churches almost invariably address the propriety of using salary to reward or punish staff during annual reviews. Their boards are more likely to be composed of high-achieving professionals used to such business systems. Is it proper, though, to use material awards as compensation for commendable ministerial performance? For instance, is one minister truly worth a greater salary than another in God's kingdom?

Worth is not the same as value. God's children share a similar worth as image bearers. For the loving Father, the prodigal was of no less worth than the elder son. Only Christ is truly worthy, and our worthiness is complete only by being in him. As members of his body, all humans are equal. But to an institution, such as the church, people's value differs according to the use of their various gifts.

We established a salary scale that was similar for educators with various degrees and experience who teach in the local public schools. Each level had its own low and high limits. A staff member's advancement on the scale was determined annually by his or her value to the church, but always within the limits. We related salary to performance because each staff member was hired to carry an agreed-on part of the ministerial responsibilities of the church.

The level of mutual trust and fairness between the board and the staff members can greatly affect them and the church. Staff members need to know how they are being evaluated and compensated—and why. All staff members, board members, and congregants need to see that actual performance matters and will be used fairly for determining compensation. Yet because of issues of privacy and perhaps jealousy, it is wise to include only one summary figure for staff salaries in the annual budget, which is distributed as part of the agenda for the annual congregational meeting.

Still, using salaries to reward good results and discourage poor effort should have limits. What about someone who simply cannot do his or her work adequately, or who cannot get along well with others? We reviewed and confirmed all possible terminations, discussing them with appropriate staff members, board members, the senior pastor, and the direct supervisor. We explained the reasons for termination, summarized records of past discussions and annual employee reviews, and emphasized and explained how the action taken was in the interest of both the staff member and the church. We always provided adequate and fair separation pay and professional counseling, along with relocation assistance. Usually we asked the person to leave the church position immediately. If the preceding reviews and support were properly provided, the immediate termination would not be a surprise.

Sometimes the employee would not accept the group's explanation and decision. Also, his or her friends on staff were invited to review nonconfidential facts if they felt that an employee had been mistreated. Occasionally the terminated employee would leave angrily. But most of the time there was little disagreement beyond a few legitimate questions, since earlier reviews had explained and recorded the issues causing termination.

We tried to go the long mile by helping with professional counseling, which often resulted in the former employee landing a better-fitting position elsewhere. In one case, a former staff member benefited so much by leaving us that he returned years later and thanked me for insisting that he would be far happier and more productive in another type of ministry. He has since become a recognized ministry leader. A church should always try to turn a negative hire into a positive result for the kingdom. Otherwise, everyone suffers, including the congregation.

Conclusion

The suburban church can learn much about staffing by welcoming the insights and experiences of members who learned about the topic from business and nonprofit endeavors. Although corporate models are not perfectly suitable to the church, they offer considerable benefits when applied discerningly with love.

Church ministers and other staff are spiritual as well as "human" resources. By serving one another in love, they also serve the congregation. They can thrive on proper fellowship, encouragement, assessment, and rewards. Staffing mistakes are inevitable but significantly unavoidable. Moreover, reviewing staff efforts helps prevent a church from getting carried away by the latest theological, educational, evangelistic, and worship fads. A staff-wise suburban church has to know who it is as well as who and how it serves. It does not depend on others to do its work. It enjoys fellowship, even play, because the staff does, too.

Discussion Questions

1. What do your staff job descriptions suggest about your church vision and priorities?
2. How has your church used business models appropriately or inappropriately to review staff and their programs?
3. How has your staff modeled joyful fellowship for the congregation? How could it do so even more effectively?

Chapter Seven

Engaging Society

Years ago the Director General of the World Health Organization and President of the World Federation for Mental Health gave a widely quoted speech claiming that Christian missionaries deceived the Eskimos. According to news media, he argued that Christians had wrongly invaded the culture of those otherwise happy people and had made them miserable by telling them that they were sinners. The Eskimos supposedly never knew that they were sinners and therefore never felt guilty until outsiders introduced the idea of sin to their culture. He opined that the missionaries should have left the Eskimos alone.

At the time, I wondered if he also would claim that a suburb is better off without an historic church anchored in biblical teaching about sin. Would suburbanites live more contentedly without even knowing that salvation is an option? Is the gospel ever a detriment to their own or others' mental health?

These are ridiculous questions for some Christians. But they had become part of public discourse beyond the conversations among mental health experts and anthropologists. I felt that as a suburban pastor I needed to face them honestly on behalf of both Christians and nonbelievers in the community as well as in our congregation. So I decided to speak up.

Going Public

I did not realize it fully, but by going public I was reaching beyond the church to the broader community of largely educated people who want to know if the Christian faith really has something to say about life. Suburbanites, in particular, generally seek practical but defensible opinions about social issues. Like others, they live and work among schools, businesses, and governments that provide practical services. Suburbanites aptly wonder about the ideas and theories behind such services: Do such institutions currently serve society? How can they serve more effectively?

I first expressed my concerns about the speech on a local radio show. Listener phone calls and later comments expressed to me personally showed that others were concerned, too. I was discovering that going public with the implications of the gospel, engaging the community on topics related to the news of the day, and doing so respectfully without self-righteous rhetoric were changing how the community viewed me and our church. Soon *we* were being asked questions and even consulted by members of the broader community. Clearly we had discovered something about suburban ministry.

Like the apostle Paul at Mars Hill, I had listened to the opinion leaders of the day and then responded plainly and honestly. I was simply trying to enter public discourse faithfully, remaining sensitive to others' perceptions and assumptions.

Soon I was asked to testify before a committee of the Illinois legislature in Springfield regarding the underlying philosophy of what seemed to be a largely secular, overly confident mental health movement. Caught up in the possible benefits of society-wide mental health assessment, the state legislature had introduced a bill that would establish a system for all schools to employ child psychologists to observe and record the behavior of each child in grades 1–5. This requirement supposedly would ensure that future generations of state citizens would be free of guilt feelings since children could thereby be managed into happiness through therapy rather than suffer guilt through personal accountability. If asked to do so, how could I not speak up publicly, even in the halls of government?

Tackling Church-State Issues

To many Christians, this bill and its underlying faith in popular therapy was an intolerable departure from the church's historic moral and theological convictions. How could the church stand on the sidelines as some psychologists and politicians questioned the value of any guilt or conscience? How could I, as a shepherd of a growing, well-informed suburban flock, let my own members potentially support a political movement based on utopian social engineering—without being accused of rejecting all psychology and counseling? I accepted speaking engagements at numerous meetings of concerned parents and several service organizations. I also wrote a cover story for *Christianity Today* titled "Do Humanists Exploit Our Tensions?"

Having gone beyond the local radio audience, I was engaging the wider culture that my church members and our surrounding community was already discussing. I was, at first without realizing it, becoming the kind of pastor they needed and prized. Yet I was also starting to walk a fine line between ministry and political advocacy. Virtually every suburban church ends up having to walk such a line as the pastor or members engage the wider society.

This kind of socially oriented ministry of discernment was rarely practiced in my Christian tradition. My denomination was fairly ethnic and tribal, often concerned more with internal matters than with the "world," except for foreign and sometimes urban missionary efforts. After all, many members reasoned, missionaries were the ones paid to interact with "secular" society.

The mental health controversy birthed in me a new calling that broadened my horizons far beyond my local congregation. When the bill lost by a large margin, I had to wonder what would have happened if no one had spoken up against it. Was I being overly concerned? Should I have ignored the issue—at least publicly? If I had not addressed it publicly, what would have occurred? I felt like

I had become aware of a minister's broader calling as an ambassador to the wider world, even the intersection of church and state.

According to many conservative and liberal church leaders, parish pastors may address social issues from the pulpit and sometimes even announce a more-or-less-official church stance to the broader community. Since the issue of required psychological testing of children was heating up in our community, it was already generating discussion in my congregation and eliciting political support in opposition to the bill. I did not create the public issue as much as I simply addressed the emerging discourse about it. Certainly my public stance offered me and our church a higher profile, but I did not get involved primarily for the publicity. I was not trying to create a social movement. I decided not to use my pulpit to "campaign" for or against the bill, but I would use the public discourse about the bill to address the perils of secularism in psychology and other professions.

Today there are many high-profile, morally discerning watchdog organizations that monitor local, state, and national politics for signs of antireligious movements and legislation. On the conservative side especially, many evangelical churches back such groups. Parachurch organizations also solicit support for or opposition to legislative agendas. No one should argue against their rights to do so, as long as such groups stay within the laws affecting nonprofit groups' and churches' involvement in social and political issues. But what lines should be drawn to prevent suburban churches from becoming largely political entities where the gospel is preached primarily for the sake of raising political funds and advocating political causes?

Involving the Congregation?

Since I was a fairly new pastor of a recently organized, independent church who lacked both related experience and advice from a larger ecclesiastical body, we were on our own without clear guidance. I wondered then as I did many times later, Should I encourage my congregation to engage society? What biblical insights could help a church and pastor that felt called to a community ministry? Was "going public" good for the pastor and the congregation in the long run?

I reviewed the biblical and historical understandings of the purposes of the Christian church, hoping to give sound guidance as we ventured increasingly into public life. First, it seemed clear that Christians should be aware of and civilly oppose all those movements or laws that foster unchristian behavior. On the one hand, the church has to respect the freedom of nonbelievers to live according to their own consciences. On the other hand, when unchristian ways of life are being codified in the laws of the land, Christians need to speak up, making their case as civilly and persuasively as possible. In today's world, all kinds of nonreligious groups advocate for social issues, so the church has to be careful not to come across as just one more political movement. Yet the church must help believers understand and live in accordance with their faith as supported in the Scripture.

Second, Christians should be able to speak with a unified voice on basic moral matters because of their loyalty to Christ and their shared biblical teachings. Unlike society in general, which is riddled with disparate voices and competing special-interest groups, the church ought to be able to articulate at a foundational level a common voice in favor of such biblical themes as peace, truth, and justice. If churches become informed, speak in moderation, and focus on the basics, they have a unique ability to speak univocally to the local and national conscience.

Of course sin enters the picture, creating divisions. Also, many issues are complex and can be addressed in a variety of ways. In the case of cutting-edge ethical issues resulting from technological innovation, for instance, the church probably should clarify the issues rather than pretend to have "the answer." Nevertheless, the church's overall historical record of speaking up, more or less in unity, includes marvelous examples of speaking the truth prophetically even though churches were divided. Among the best examples are the ways that most churches opposed slavery and eventually favored civil rights.

Since the church is not a political entity, however, it has to avoid getting overly tangled in civic affairs, or it might lose its root spiritual mission. The church is not called to manufacture heaven on earth. Augustine rightly distinguished between the City of God and the City of Man. This distinction is especially important for suburban congregations composed of some people who are used to having and leveraging power in business, nonprofit organizations, and perhaps governmental affairs. It is critically important to keep in mind that Christians' primary political influence should be as individual citizens and as members of extrachurch groups, not as an ecclesiastical unit.

Moreover, individual church members should be active in society for the sake of the common good, not purely for self-interest. We wanted our new church to support members who felt called to get involved in civil government, school boards, social justice and environmental movements, and similar causes that can bless and nurture local communities and the world. Yet we needed to make sure that the church nurtured the kinds of believers who could speak wisely and well in society, with moderation and respect for their adversaries on behalf of the common good. Churches must not only evangelize but also instruct members in living out their faith in a way that will enable them to effectively influence the culture and its institutions. Only then can a Christ-centered congregation's members wisely penetrate all the areas of life in the wider community.

Frankly, this is a problem in many suburban churches. Well-intentioned clergy and lay leaders too quickly jump on the latest moral campaign or political bandwagon that they learn about on Christian broadcasts or in mass mailings sent to churches by parachurch groups that are quick to speak up in society and slow to listen and study the issues at stake. It is easy to insert such organizations' alarmist materials into the weekly bulletin and feel like the congregation is thereby socially active and wise. I understand how this happens in busy suburban churches where pastors and lay leaders have a passion for social action but little time to become informed.

The opposite is also common. Relatively wise and discerning members are either discouraged from community and civic involvement or they see the City of God as the only, or at least the most important, calling in their lives. They cannot imagine that politics, for example, is a worthy calling except possibly for full-time politicians.

Developing a World-and-Life View

An active church member cautiously said to me, "If I become a member of the village board I will have to drop out of my Bible study group." To her surprise, I encouraged her to drop out of the Bible study group and serve the village. She had been born and raised in Lutheran churches, had studied catechism, and had committed her life to Christ. She knew much about living faithfully. Her family was doing well in the church. How many Bible studies did she think she had to attend before she was ready to serve faithfully outside the church?

The basic biblical truth of neighborly service to others had never struck her as a reason for social action. Somehow she had picked up the idea that faith is almost exclusively a matter of personal sanctification. She had wrongly acquiesced to an individualistic notion that personal spirituality is all that matters in living faithfully. For her, studying Scripture was a more saintly thing to do than serving on the village board. She held an impoverished world-and-life view.

A suburban church needs to engage society beyond just domestic and foreign missions. Only some suburban residents will enter a church building. Evangelism cannot possibly be the sole external goal of a congregation, or it will never truly penetrate its community and equip its members to be caring, loving, Christ-like ambassadors beyond its sanctuary walls. Evangelistic campaigns do not necessarily produce an outwardly focused, socially engaged congregation, whereas a broadly engaged church that dialogues with, as well as works within, the community is already practicing authentic outreach in tune with a robust world-and-life view.

A dynamic, service-oriented church will not be ignored by the local community. People will know about it, and it will attract residents as long as it is addressing real wounds and concerns beyond its doors. In fact, a congregation that humbly seeks to serve will say and do some things in the community through its members that no other institution can. This is why sociologists have been able to document the incredible social capital that churches and synagogues invariably provide for communities.

Moreover, the line between service and witness often is wonderfully thin even when the congregation is humbly upholding its own members in public forums. I saw this firsthand when a few members of our church were on the local high school swim team, which had a legacy of winning major swimming events. Out of a good desire to keep up the fine record, the coach announced that the varsity team would begin practicing on Sunday mornings. When the members who belonged to our congregation met to discuss the issue, however, they decided to protest. So they met with the coach and explained that they attended church on Sunday morning and could not meet as required. The coach found this unimaginable and warned that they would have to be dropped from the team.

These brave teenagers preempted the coach, indicating that they would regretfully resign from the team. Further amazed, the coach asked how they could even think of such a drastic response. He wanted to know what was so important about Sunday morning "church." They invited him to find out by joining the team members for worship. Not wanting to lose his best swimmers, he agreed to attend the following Sunday and afterward make a decision on the team's fate.

He came. He heard. He saw. Christ conquered! Our young people remained on his team. The coach and his wife joined our church. The team continued winning without Sunday morning practice. Perhaps out of respect and admiration for the coach, these swimmers served him, the school, and the community as real champions. One of them went on to win in the next Olympics.

Although this story is exceptional, it demonstrates the two critically important aspects of the church's broader vision that often distinguish it from other institutions. First, the church needs to empathize with those in its community who face difficult situations, issues, and choices. We understood and acknowledged the coach's predicament. The school board, staff, administrators, and parents wanted a winning team and were willing to give their time and resources toward that end. The coach was on the line.

Second, the church must support its empathy with excellent action, not flowery promises and mediocre follow-up. Rather than just caring *about* others, it needs to care *for* them with all of the abilities at its disposal. When the coach saw personally the kind of community we had within the church, he, too, wanted to be cared about and cared for by excellent as well as empathetic servants. And the young swimmers gave him their all, attending additional practices on other days as needed. In the end, neither the church nor the school was willing to settle for second best.

When I addressed on the radio the issue of state-mandated psychological testing in public schools, and began speaking on the topic at other churches and civic groups, my witness had the same effect as the swimming episode. Responding to the news reports, interested residents visited and joined the church. They were attracted to a thoughtful theological position with moral integrity. Some of them invited their unchurched adult children to learn the biblical basis for healthy and productive living, including how to address guilt rather than pretend it is merely a social invention. In many cases these adult children and their older offspring became believers who modeled the loving Christian family, where grace truly reduced excessive guilt and where personal consciences were nurtured.

Yet we avoided politicizing our congregation. We did not integrate this issue into the church's programs. Some members of a suburban church will want to use the church as a pulpit for specific social and political agendas—such as whom to vote for and which legislation to support or oppose. Surely members can—and should—discuss particular social issues. As a pastor, I also had a civic obligation to care for those who might be affected by the state legislation. But as soon as our pulpit witness became primarily political, we had probably stepped from the City of God into the City of Man, potentially turning the church itself into an arm of one or another special-interest group.

As people visited our church because of members' public stands on moral issues, they heard the broader message of Christian faith, not a political "gospel." They discovered that morality, like so many public stands on other great virtues in society, becomes especially meaningful when it is anchored in a deeper, foundational relationship with God and God's people.

Our witness to visitors made clear that there is a major difference between being socially engaged because of one's faith and letting one's faith be co-opted by activists who sometimes care only about winning. I saw activists assuming extreme positions just to attract media attention. Modest, balanced positions rarely made the news. I had to remain on guard and encourage others from our congregation to do so as well. We needed to ask ourselves, Why are we speaking publicly—what is our deepest motive? How are others perceiving our language and actions? What kinds of persons are we working with? Are they respected members of the community?

For instance, my public position regarding the mental health movement triggered the attention of McCarthyesque fanatics who traded in fear and innuendo. They even became active in our church and aggressively promoted their agendas supposedly as compatible with a Christian witness. I and others should have expected this, since my public stance as a minister could have been used by any group to gain its own public legitimacy. Moreover, this fear-mongering group seemed to support the church's biblical vision that God is sovereign in every area of life. But to them, the City of God and the City of Man were identical. They saw Jesus' church as a political entity and wanted us to endorse and support their political agendas.

The Church and the Kingdom

The real task of the local church is calling and equipping people to be loyal citizens of the kingdom of God, not to train members primarily for political action. Christ did not die to save people for heavenly bliss so that they could engage in social or political movements on earth. God calls people into the church so that they can learn with fear and trembling as well as with joy and perseverance what it means to faithfully prepare for God's reign on earth as in heaven. Believers will sometimes disagree about how to translate their faith into social engagement beyond the walls of the church even as they share faith in the same triune God.

Humans cannot create heaven on earth any more than they can create heaven in the suburbs. This world fell into disrepair when God's image bearers arrogantly tried to appropriate the future from God. Utopian social campaigns are just schemes, regardless of how well they are couched in religious rhetoric. Surely God is redeeming the world through the work of his faithful, redeemed image bearers. But any church that concentrates excessively on human effort rather than divine grace forgets that there is a greater "Mission beyond the Mission."

Nevertheless, culture and society are denied their greater potential when the church focuses only on itself, as if Christ established the church merely for heavenly purposes. Suburban congregations especially need to recall Jesus' mandate to go *into* all the world, or they will become victims of the very demographic shifts that gave rise to the suburban attitudes of separation, exclusivism, and superiority. Too many suburbanites see their newer, cleaner, island communities as closer to heaven on earth, without urban conflicts among racial and ethnic groups and supposedly free of crime and poverty. The fact is that conflicts and crime simply take different forms, such as zoning battles and white-collar fraud.

Without this broader, all-encompassing understanding of the fall, suburban congregations and sometimes entire denominations may feel the luxury to focus on their own affairs without worrying about the less fortunate people "in the city." For some, sending money to support foreign missionaries has become their only significant social action, practiced safely from a distance. Meanwhile, youth groups can turn into mini social clubs that send teenagers to mission fields too often, as though they are mere tourists. Busyness itself does not guarantee a suburban church's external vision.

A suburban church that renews its mission as a socially and culturally active body of saints, equipped for lay as well as clerical ministry in the world, is the only solution for such misguided separatism. We were blessed to understand this when we launched Christ Church as the only congregation in our village. We imagined the church biblically as an epicenter of community involvement, welcoming all residents who did not attend as well as those who did. This is the only vision of the suburban church that avoids either tribalism, on the one hand, or balkanization, on the other. For all of their good features, some megachurches have fallen into the latter problem, wrongly equating the church community with a collection of internally focused "ministries" that address dozens of special-interest groups—from being single to losing weight— but failing to *be* the church in the general ministry of community involvement.

The local congregation is most healthy when it looks outward, pursuing its greater mission beyond its tribal interests. If it does not do this, it turns inward, dissipating its energies on the administration of its programs, on who gets credit, on building new buildings, and on trying merely to keep church life peaceful. This pattern generally leads to petty internal conflict, anxiety, and spiritual stagnation even if the church is growing numerically and creating an impressive architectural facade for its public identity.

The personal analogy is telling. Psychologists have discovered that a healthy individual looks outward, serves others, and becomes thankful for the opportunities of living with and for them. Even generally successful persons need such a relational, expansive vision of health. This also applies to institutions. The church has a mission to flourish beyond itself. In this sense, a spiritually healthy congregation is well, not neurotic; dynamic, not static; humble, not proud; loving, not selfish; generous, not greedy.

A Spiritual Home

We discovered that the suburban church has to competently equip members in at least three ways if it expects to be a healthy, socially engaged congregation. One is individual counseling, as necessary. That is time-intensive, one-on-one work in which the church personally serves individuals with specific needs, usually in particular situations or dilemmas. The goal is not to provide a full complement of services available through psychiatrists and other professionals, but instead to address more immediate, usually spiritually related crises and life complications. Perhaps the primary purpose will be to develop a specific person's awareness of the presence of God amidst confusion, doubt, or uncertainty. Suburban busyness, in particular, creates a need for people to slow down and rediscover that God is indeed God, and that even type-A personalities with abundant resources cannot save the world themselves.

Second is the need for healthy groups within which critically important friendships and mutual service can emerge organically, even though the group structures are established for educational and other purposes by the church staff. Children and young people, for instance, need to know that they have love and support from others in the church even though most of their lives during the week are based on extrachurch relationships. A suburban congregation can foster other relational groups as well, such as new mothers, retirees, singles, and people who have similar life situations and only differ because of individual traits or experiences. But these kinds of groups need to encourage participants' wider congregational involvement in order to be healthy, spiritually transformative, open, outreach-oriented groups. Once they begin substituting for "church," they lose the broader vision, fall into cliques, and typically suffer from petty jealousies and disputes.

Third, adult church membership is more than mere "attendance." Here again, some suburban congregations fail because of their infatuation with purely numerical growth. Teaching cultural and social discernment is no easier than modeling it, especially when there are likely to be reasonable differences of informed opinion about how to relate faith to actual community needs and services. There is no sense in rehashing tired old questions about the social gospel or about good works versus grace, or even about evangelism versus neighborly service. The real issues have to do with authentic Christian engagement that is simultaneously witness and service. Since some congregations will be more gifted than others at particular tasks as well as at forms of discernment, churches should be open to the multiplicity of congregational interests, talents, gifts, age levels, vocation, marital status, and the like without ever letting such categories exclusively define the congregation's self-identity.

Christians will always have to work carefully to define what mature thought and action are in such areas as economics, government, health, education, and justice. The church can give members doctrinal and biblical language as basic tools, but if leaders become overly dogmatic about how to apply such tools they can snuff out creative ideas and squelch new forms of social engagement. Social problems change over time, so solutions need to evolve as well. What might it mean to be pro-life in the widest and deepest sense? To engage in prison ministry that restores offenders and victims alike? To oppose specific legislation while remaining hopeful about the positive role of government in providing "common grace"? To feed the hungry without making them dependent on handouts?

Faithful suburban churches need to ask these kinds of questions to make sure that they have not merely accepted hackneyed answers concocted by extrachurch self-interest groups. The more and varied the congregational participation in such church-based self-education, the better. The goal should not be to answer such perplexing questions once and for all, but to build creative kingdom citizens who will go out from the church into the world as mature, socially involved Christians doing the best they can to be both salt and light.

The church, then, is like a home for nurturing new and old Christians, to bring insights, assistance, and encouragement to those who suffer as a result of the world's deep brokenness. Believers come usually to get nourished and strengthened, or simply by the compulsion of the Holy Spirit. Once inside the church, however, they should see ever more deeply that they have been called to serve others within and beyond the congregation. The work will consider different people's talents both within and beyond the suburban church tribe.

Conclusion

My congregation and I learned about the value and perils of faith-based social engagement. One political group managed to take over our board and threatened to fire me if I did not resign. They were convinced that the nation's anticommunist crusade should define the church's social witness. In the end, they were the ones to leave our church as cooler heads and more discerning members also spoke up.

As my efforts in Illinois against mandated school psychological testing showed, however, it is possible to be involved in public discourse even as a church leader without turning the church into a political party. The democratic gift of social engagement can be a blessing for church and society as long as churches keep this distinction in mind. In addition to humility, suburban churches need a robust world-and-life view that transcends mere politics on behalf of the common good rather than just one or another political party or social movement.

Discussion Questions

1. What sociopolitical issues have caused conflicts within your church, and how have you tried to heal any rifts?
2. How and how well does your church encourage members' social engagement without becoming a political entity?
3. How can your church's preaching and education foster a robust Christian world-and-life view that includes a distinction between the City of God and the City of Man?

Chapter Eight

Crafting a Global Vision

At six o'clock in the morning the screech of wild turkeys having their necks wrung awakened me. I had been sleeping on two wooden benches pushed together in the sanctuary of a small frame church in the Chol territory of rural Chiapas, Mexico. After arriving the previous evening, I was welcomed by our missionary and his wife, who apologetically shared their precious canned food. Their garage-like home contained a mattress in one corner, an open clothesline for their wardrobe in another corner, a table, two chairs, and a crate for a third person to sit on.

After a brief visit with them, I was led by flashlights to their church building about a hundred yards away. Two native men were already snoring there in the darkness. They had walked that entire day to participate in the same ceremony the next day that had brought me two thousand miles from Chicago. Now, as the turkeys screeched and the morning sun shone, I realized that my snoring companions were already gone as I was abruptly brought back to consciousness in the real world of Wycliffe Bible translators in southern Mexico. We had much to celebrate—because the translators had completed translating and publishing the Bible into the Chol language. I was there to represent the suburban congregation that had provided the major support for the project.

The God of All People

During my two-day visit to rural Chiapas, I witnessed firsthand the work of those whom God calls to serve in other cultures. In terms of material wealth, my home church represented the top few percent of all people in the world. But when it came to whom God loves, and who loves God, both suburban Chicago and rural Mexico are fertile ground for the work of the Holy Spirit. The mind and heart of Jesus embrace all people made in the image and likeness of a compassionate, empathetic God.

How can a suburban congregation keep this in mind, especially when so few of its members are likely to see what I had just observed? How can a suburban church bless those in other cultures and be blessed by them? Only by reaching out in love and meekness to other parts of the world, learning as well as teaching. We were not sure where our commitment would lead us, but we knew that crosscultural service is a necessary sign of spiritual life in the all-too-insular suburbs. The heart of every true church, including those in comfortable suburbs, must beat for the redemption of the world. Otherwise a congregation is not really a church.

Fostering Suburban Gratitude

As a suburban pastor, I often wondered why I had been called to serve in such a privileged time and place while some of my seminary colleagues in "foreign" missions seemed to suffer daily hardship and inconveniences. I saw their children often feeling torn between two or more cultures. I heard about these missionaries' fears, anxiety, loneliness, and doubts about their effectiveness. Yet I also witnessed their joy and delight, and especially their gratefulness in the midst of their trials.

So in spite of my congregation's relative affluence, I promised God and myself that I would do all I could to support and present the cause of missions to parishes that could support such self-sacrificial endeavors. A suburban church has to be crossculturally engaged, even evangelistically supportive. If it is not, the congregation is much more likely to become self-satisfied, even ungrateful.

St. Theresa of Calcutta was known the world over for having been a living example of her mandate to all who would listen: "Do something beautiful for God." There are many special people in the world who walk in her footprints—joyous, loving, self-denying, "beautiful" persons. Many are missionaries. They volunteer to live for Jesus and to take up residence in nearly all cultures and hemispheres. They are among the most dedicated, wise, and hospitable agents of God. I can testify personally to the incomparable value of traveling across and around the earth to spend time with them. They inspire and renew others' energy for the spread and practice of the Christian faith. They document the declaration of Scripture that it is more blessed to give than to receive. No persons on earth have greater peace of mind and heart, more wealth of soul and spirit, than most missionaries. They are living saints from whom we all need to learn.

This is why suburbanites need to do more than merely support missionaries with financial and prayer offerings. Suburbanites should put on a missionary spirit, thereby reflecting in their own lives the heart and life of humble, faithful, grateful servants. Not every suburban believer can go overseas to witness missions firsthand, but all can meet with missionaries in their suburban homes and churches. Such meetings can stir suburbanites' hearts and souls with the inner joy of reaching the world for Jesus. The resulting blessings can far outweigh any costs of time or resources.

Missionary Vision versus Selfish Myopia

The alternative to a missionary spirit, especially in suburban churches, is petty pride, negativity, or at best indifference to the rest of the world beyond the manicured lawns, groomed country clubs, flowery parties, and well-lit shopping malls. Congregations that focus on themselves tend to implode. They can even become havens for self-pitying, complaining people. Their world can shrink so much that it revolves only around them, destroying the luster and beauty of life wherever they go. By overly focusing on the alleged superiority of their own ways of life, they can suffocate their spirits.

Without an outward, neighbor-loving perspective, congregations resemble feuding little groups of immature children. They become places for self-fulfilling critics and naysayers who demonstrate rigid, legalistic thinking and ungrateful living. Such churches become monuments to themselves. Consider this analogy from suburban retailing: When merchants spend their time rearranging merchandise, deciding who gets the credit and profit, and arguing about how the store will function, the customers will feel like they are expendable and will probably leave. Eventually, we all reap what we sow.

Missionary activities, a missions-oriented heart, and missionaries themselves are all gifts to the givers, too. They can help rescue a self-satisfied, spiritually claustrophobic church from itself. Churches ought not to do missions because it makes them feel good about themselves; that would be the wrong motivation. When they do missions with the right, loving hearts, respectful of those with whom they share the gospel, however, churches are blessed. Missions-minded churches benefit from being biblical, from following the example as well as the command of Jesus Christ to go into the world and baptize in his name. The book of Acts, in particular, describes this aspect of being a church. It also describes the incredible fact that the apostle Paul found joy in "all things," including persecution and prison, because he was a witness to the love of God, the life of Jesus, and the work of the Spirit in the world. He did not have the time or inclination to be a myopic complainer or to be self-satisfied with his work.

Engaging Members and Nonmembers

We developed a worldwide missions program partly to stretch our perception of the kingdom of God beyond "foreign" evangelism and church planting. Missions venues could include everything from our comfortable, upper-middle-class neighborhoods to inner-city youth outreach and prison ministries. Our task was to gain suburban ownership of programs and the people whose work would promote peace and justice as well as evangelism.

Hoping to avoid becoming so intent on our own congregational activities that we would end up working to capacity before broadening our missional horizons, we began our world outreach six months after founding the congregation. At that stage, many nonmembers were attending our services. Some of them were new to the Christian faith, while others were either unhappy with or inactive at other churches; in both cases, they were coming to us afresh, open to a new vision of congregational life and missionary practices. Even if they were uncertain of their own loyalties to Christ and the church's historic mandates, they were interested in the common good. For instance, they expected the church to be involved in the work of serving the disadvantaged in society. Their desire to help others was our entrée.

With an announcement on the religious page of the local newspaper, we invited everyone in the church or community to an open meeting where they could learn how a spoken language is converted to writing for the purpose of advancing world literacy. They would get to see an expert with more than twenty-five years in the field demonstrate how this is done. At the meeting, our invited translator from Wycliffe Bible Translators explained his lifelong work with the natives who lived on the shores of the Amazon River. We also served lunch as an expression of our hospitality.

Since many suburbanites are interested in education, specialized skills, and world affairs, we expected that such a program would attract not only our members but also their neighbors. Clearly the session was implicitly Christian and even evangelistic with respect to the efforts of Wycliffe to translate Scripture. Nevertheless, literacy can have tremendous benefits for any culture as it addresses the educational needs of members in areas such as health care and law. Few areas of the world are unaffected by other, more developed societies—for good or for bad. These kinds of common interests brought together a fairly diverse suburban audience and demonstrated the humanitarian aspects of missions. After a fascinating demonstration of his expertise, including his sensitivity to native culture, the translator had earned the opportunity to tell how translating and reading the Bible in native tongues can also bless and transform human lives. As he indicated, translating Scripture provides an opportunity for other cultures to consider Jesus' claims for themselves, in their own ways.

The attendees themselves asked how this particular organization began, and why. In this case, Wycliffe's work clearly had both humanitarian and spiritual benefits that were easy to demonstrate: this Amazonian culture previously practiced headhunting and cannibalism. Relating the gospel to their own culture, they had given up these practices in favor of peace and forgiveness. They were "free" to embrace the kind of justice Jesus proclaimed in the Sermon on the Mount. This remarkable story of grace moved those who attended to offer the initial gifts to support a budding worldwide mission program. Our fledgling church had laid a building block for its own role in worldwide missions. Suddenly we had a missions program and budget—before we had even plans for our own building.

Although this was our first effort toward becoming a deeply missional congregation, we quickly realized that our underlying principles were both biblical and suburban friendly. We gained the attention and support of a community of attendees that included believers, skeptics, and the curious. And we did so in a way that was true to the mandate of Christ, intellectually respectable, inspirational, and noncontroversial. We were not going to let ourselves get sidetracked by doctrinal fine points, arguments about whether the church should support *either* social justice *or* evangelism.

Our job was to locate and support people who were sensitive to such issues but not overly encumbered or driven by them. For all of these reasons, we knew that suburbanites' first impression of our mission program was critical to our future emphasis on reaching out to the world. The informed people who lived in our suburb often were world citizens: they would recognize if our church lacked integrity. Thanks to the Wycliffe translator, his fascinating presentation had set our sails for the irresistible winds of the Holy

Spirit with a boat full of supporters, who included visionary people beyond the small harbor of our newly launched church.

From this small but auspicious beginning, some of our early members felt called to far deeper waters. They sought to learn more about church missions programs and to formalize our emerging efforts. Trustees asked a group to define its missional purpose, serving as a new committee to propose a mission program to our board of elders. This group wisely set the parameters and administrative policies for years to come.

Organizing for Action

In typical suburban style, we included "due diligence" regarding a missions program in our long-range plan. We appointed committee members who were accustomed to working within organized structures, asking them to guide us in the administration and oversight of the missionaries we might support. They discerned that our independent church should not become a mission agency for the administration of missionaries and their assignments. Doing so would lead us into such potential issues as conduct liability, governmental employment reports, health-care provisions, and retirement policies and administration. Instead the group concluded that the church should work with established mission agencies of relatively compatible theological commitments, sound financial policies, accountability, integrity, and established reputation. The major theological issue for us was ensuring that evangelism would be part of the missionaries' work. There were plenty of other organizations that would focus solely on social and economic efforts. We sought outreach for the whole person—heart, mind, body, and soul.

Missionary Missteps and Policies

We stumbled early, as our enthusiasm overcame our decision making. Eager to give our own grammar school children a cross-cultural summer camp experience beyond what was available locally, we sent a small group of them to an established church program of Native Americans in Northern Wisconsin. Before long, congregational parents were calling the church office to request that we bring home their children. As we soon discovered, our church's children were being taught at this camp that Christians did not use lipstick, wear shorts, or color their fingernails. Not having done our homework adequately, we had placed congregational children in a legalistic setting that led to the condemnation of them and their parents, friends, and relatives. Our offspring were even isolated from other children at the camp, resulting in troubling conflicts.

Another difficulty arose when one of our first foreign missionaries became seriously ill. The mission agency through which we supported him pointed out that they had no hospitalization insurance covering their missionaries and refused to assume medical responsibility. Fortunately, one of our medical doctors and his wife, who was a nurse, took him into their home and treated him for several weeks until he could return overseas. We learned by experience that careful scrutiny of mission agencies is fundamental to safe, productive mission programs.

These and other experiences led us to the following operational policies:

1. We would only support persons who were related to a reputable mission agency that met our criteria.
2. All mission agencies represented must submit to us their budgets, statements of faith, and names of their boards of directors.
3. Support would be granted only to those persons and causes that were clear in their faith regarding Jesus Christ and their evangelistic commitment to missions.
4. We would never support more than a minority dollar amount of a missionaries' annual budget as established by that person's board.
5. We would only support persons who would appear for a personal interview and meet our criteria.

6. Every person we would support would have to present his/her work to the congregation in person.

7. Accountability required an annual review to determine the continuation of the relationship and budget. Term limits of support were clearly stated.

8. Mission personnel or organizations supported by our church would not be allowed to solicit directly from church members.

9. The mission committee would report to the board of elders and submit an annual budget for approval.

10. The mission committee would have its own treasurer and keep books compatible with 1) the financial system used by the congregation's general treasurer, and 2) agreed-on auditing practices.

11. To insure personal relationships, we supported mission institutions only by supporting the individuals (such as administrators) who communicated with us.

12. Humanitarian causes without a gospel witness would not qualify for mission support.

Mapping Mission's Terrain

Given our limited funding, we realized that we had to define the area or groups for our missions' locales. We considered everything outside our parish area, looking especially at existing members' interests, such as projects at the county jail and in the inner city, and minority benevolence in the Chicago area. As mission agencies heard about us, we received additional applications from needy groups in the area.

Soon we realized that our efforts were too concentrated, so we intentionally expanded worldwide. Noting that Christian nationals were far more successful than Western missionaries at reaching their citizens, we preferred funding those who had grown up with and were respected among the groups they served. They generally understood the cultural and linguistic idioms, and were sympathetic to historical influences of religious traditions. They were also far more economical to support than "foreign" missionaries from North America. This cultural sensitivity prepared us to anticipate many outreach practices that were not then commonly supported in the United States. Long before it was popular to do so, we supported endeavors around the world that were contextualizing the faith with and for natives.

Our committee also considered the variety of "missions." We were open to supporting the culturally sensitive, classical missionary who plants churches, calls people to repentance, and asks for commitments to Jesus Christ. At the same time, however, we needed to broaden our holistic support to include native educators, teachers, translators, medical caregivers, servants of the poor, orphans, the abused, and even administrators, pilots, service personnel, and others whose efforts round out the purposes of peace and justice as well as evangelism.

After several years, we succeeded in establishing a reasonably balanced mission program in all of these categories. We excitedly became part of the kingdom of God as it initiates and sustains a worldwide community of believers and becomes part of the life and prayers of local churches through creative, extensive missional programs. To keep our program of support vibrant over time, we had to provide opportunities for multigenerational families in our church to become informed and involved. Other supporters might come and go, but our growing congregation had to know about and feel a sense of ownership of our balanced program. Not every family could prayerfully and financially support all forms of outreach, but minimally each family would personally embrace one or another project of particular interest.

The Annual Missions Festival

As our church grew, we began each mission year by sending a special newsletter early in April to all of our members, announcing our annual mission festival in May. The preceding week included Sunday school activities to help our children and young adults learn about missions. Missions would be the subject of the sermon, music, and weekly Bible study groups. New and visiting missionaries would join us for the event, staying in members' homes to help forge personal relationships.

The festival, with a special theme, began on Friday afternoon, when the missionaries arrived at the church. Each of them had a booth displaying cultural artifacts and offering educational materials about their work, including newsletters, recordings, and photos. Appropriate signage and equipment were installed for the evening events.

The missionaries and the committee gathered for a time of prayer, introductions, and instruction. We informed our missionaries that many of the people attending had never met a missionary, would like to know about missionaries' lives and work, and would be inspired by personal stories, not sermonic or theological language. The missionaries were assigned a room of their own for consecutive, thirty-minute evening presentations. We asked them to dress in the traditional clothing of the people they serve. Missionary work is serious, privileged work, but it can also be fun and inspiring, so we encouraged them to take this broader approach.

Everyone gathered in the sanctuary after a fellowship dinner. The choir sang, children performed, the missionaries were introduced, and then a special feature was presented. Features included live phone conversations with our missionaries in Africa, India, Russia, and Bolivia; interviews with special guests regarding world conditions affecting foreign and domestic missionaries; and roundtable discussions with mission agency executives. Occasionally, we borrowed a short film from a mission agency—as long as it was well produced and not excessively self-promotional.

At the close of the sanctuary meeting, high school students appeared with colored flags to guide those wearing that color on their coded name tag to a room for their first missionary presentation. After thirty minutes, the groups were ushered to the next room to meet with another missionary. When the presentations were finished, we all retired to the fellowship hall for do-it-yourself ice cream sundaes. This last evening session provided time for more personal interaction with the missionaries, leading to friendships and correspondence for years to come.

Worship on the next Lord's Day, the first Sunday of May, reconnected the congregation to the Great Commission of the risen Lord. It opened with a procession and posting of flags representing the nations being served by our missionaries. The attending missionaries left their displays to follow the flag bearers. The congregation and choir sang appropriate music. Each missionary was introduced. Finally, a verbally gifted missionary would preach an inspirational message.

All of this Sunday's and previous days' activities led up to the annual Faith Promise Offering, which highlighted the needs and opportunities expressed throughout the previous week. We clarified that the entire offering would go to the field, not to the church. Members, friends, and children were all offered an opportunity to participate. Cards in the pew racks were available for those who would promise, with faith in God's blessing, to give a designated amount during the coming year. This was a promise to God, *through*, not *to* Christ Church. The card was optional. No record of the name and promise would be kept. The total of all the promises would guide the mission committee in the administration of the program and enable us to plan annual support for our missionaries. Following a prayer, a pastor or mission committee member typically offered an invitation to sign the cards, make a promise, and place the card in the offering plate.

The Holy Spirit used the festival to educate and motivate our congregation to be outreach minded as well as outreach supportive. We could not always see immediate and obvious impact in the field, but over time the Spirit-led impact gave us much about which to rejoice. Both our missionaries and congregants regularly received letters from former members who, having experienced these festivals, dedicated their own lives to the cause of world evangelism. One member unexpectedly translated and published my Basic Christianity course into Chinese; it has been used in the Far East as well as in North America. This faithful servant of God and many others are testimonials to the ongoing value of a vibrant missions program that not only financially supports missionaries but also cultivates strong ties between supporting members and those in the field.

Personal Connections

When suburban congregations prioritize missions, they find new energy, purpose, and unity. The children remember hearing about missionaries and their amazing faith and excitedly greet their missionary "friends" at a festival or during other furloughs. And they discover personally that the things taught in Sunday school really are true and make a difference throughout the world.

Having missionaries stay in their homes, eat their food, and share their experiences is always interesting as well as educational for entire families. Missionary visits bring a dimension of grace and truth to supporters, forging friendships, merging spiritual interests, and opening up life to larger meaning. Small irritants that divide and destroy congregations tend to fall away. Personal agendas and desire for credit by church staff or volunteers then have far less appeal when viewed in contrast to the selfless work of domestic and foreign missionaries. Congregational life rises to a higher standard of servanthood and stewardship than organizational structures alone could ever produce. The congregation rekindles its own soul by pursuing its call to set aside self-interest and dedicate its energies to reach the world, local and distant, with the redemptive love of God.

During my active years of parish ministry, I was often asked to define the secret of our congregational joy and growth. I was always frustrated with my reply, which inadequately described the "heart" of my answer simply by admitting that the secret is within the heart. The individual congregants' and the unified congregation's hearts must beat for Christ—for his mission, his love, and his truths. Congregational life must somehow reflect Christ's life to the world. Everything a church says and does should foster hearts that are open to his presence. Exposure to missionary work across the cultural boundaries fosters a heart of this kind. Surely it is one factor that makes a suburban congregation grow joyfully.

Becoming a Missional Teacher

Missionary hearts also help a church teacher and preacher enrich church education. There are many references in Scripture to the gods of mere wood or stone, to imaginary gods, or to gods created to serve human interests. Such gods have been influential throughout history, and still are today. In our shrinking world, they seem to be even more significant as people look to New Age philosophy and individualist religious practices. These false gods' temples populate our cities and attract many people with searching hearts.

The Lord's work progresses in strange ways as cultures and faiths collide. When our work team was in St. Petersburg, Russia, in 1990, members traded two Bibles for the opportunity to purchase cement for the floor that our team laid in the church basement. In Singapore, I conducted a Bible class of over thirty persons on a weekday afternoon. The home where we met belonged to a businessman who was working throughout the Far East. His spiritual problems centered in the ethical decisions he was compelled to make in very diverse cultural situations. He felt that the church was not giving him satisfactory training to apply biblical principles to the complex alternatives presented by non-Christian traditions. He needed personal advice, wisdom, and discernment. In short, he needed help relating "all things" to this culture without sacrificing his faith.

On another occasion, a telephone call changed the life of our congregation. It was a call from the executive secretary of the All Union Council of Evangelical Churches of the Soviet Union. He invited our radio missionary to Russia and me to preach in their major cities in 1986. We toured for three weeks under the ever-present eye of the KGB, held services from Volagrad to Leningrad and from Minsk to Moscow to standing-room-only congregations. Upon our return to Moscow, we met with the four officers of the council for debriefing. I was asked for my impressions of the churches and for my sense of the greatest need I had observed in Russia. I reported enthusiastically on Russians' depth of faith, level of spirituality, love for the Bible, and devotion to Christ. More than sixty years of restrictions and persecution had not dampened a sacrificial loyalty to the God who gave them hope.

But Bibles were scarce, seminaries were closed by the government, and Christian literature and hymn books had been burned. All that was permitted were worship services in the churches. A few laymen would share one or two Bibles and preach the sermons. The singing of memorized hymns by strong Russian voices was superb. The sermons were sincere but simplistic; often they fostered guilt, shame, fear, and legalistic judgment. They were no match for the spiritual quality of the music and the closing prayer sessions of every service. I hesitatingly and humbly critiqued the sermons, and encouraged these bold Christian leaders to make biblical and theological education available to those faithful lay preachers at the earliest opportunity. I hoped that the church under communism would somehow be able to work out these issues.

When glasnost opened the church doors in 1989, I again received a call from the council, which reminded me of my humbly critical words. Would I help them meet the need for pastoral education for their 5,000 churches? When I described this conversation to the leaders of Christ Church, they encouraged me and the chairman of our mission committee to return to Russia and try to help the emerging church meet its educational needs. Soon I was involved in concentrated travel and meetings in Russia, resulting in a plan designed to foster leadership training by correspondence courses as well as an interdenominational seminary in St. Petersburg.

Conclusion

Planting, growing, and renewing a suburban church is not just a suburban project. If a church is to become an outwardly focused congregation with its own, local missional emphasis, it needs to support and interact with those who serve in other cultures. The blessings to suburban churches resulting from such endeavors include the following:

1. Greater historical as well as contemporary practices of biblical faith and life
2. More vibrant models of Christian stewardship and values
3. A greater congregational emphasis on developing servanthood and leadership among members
4. Clearer and deeper commitments to the centrality of the simple gospel message and its life-changing power
5. An awakening awareness to the congregation's kingdom responsibilities
6. Inspiration for a church's most talented young people at a time in life when they are considering idealistic possibilities for long-term service
7. A greater sensitivity to crosscultural and especially ethical concerns
8. Enhanced confidence in the church universal, which offers the only hope for a world of brokenness
9. More attention to the Great Commission

My congregation could tell when I had recent mission experiences. I was inspired again regarding the power and veracity of our faith. I had relearned to expect the unexpected—that God is bigger than human plans and abilities. My preaching was more spacious and perhaps even more winsome, in tune with God's grace. My attitude about God's work in the world was more positive. And I, too, was less likely to get sidetracked into petty disputes within the church. How could I let that happen after meeting Mexican church leaders who walked for hours to attend our celebration, and after sharing a meal with materially poor but spiritually blessed natives who had sacrificed screeching wild turkeys in order to host even me, a suburban pastor who would return to relative luxury in *El Norte*?

Discussion Questions

1. How would you assess the missionary mind-set of your congregation?
2. How might you focus your missionary support and involvement in tune with congregants' existing interests, both domestic and international?
3. What strategies might you use to draw unchurched suburbanites into your missions projects as humanitarian as well as evangelistic ventures?

Chapter Nine

Mastering Suburban Wealth

I was driving west to a summer seminary internship in Iowa. As a hopeful pastor, I imagined myself ministering to congregations in various churches along the way. Just east of the Fox River stood a beautiful old stone church that had recently been given to a denomination. How inspired I was, just contemplating ministry in such a magnificent setting!

Years later, I befriended a local pastor who had been transferred to the very stone church that had caught my eye and stirred my budding ministerial imagination. As it turned out, however, the congregation occupying the fine-looking building was failing because of a lack of parish commitment and loyalty. The well-endowed congregation needed little cash; consequently, few donations were offered. Members saw church attendance and parish participation as optional. They had become mere consumers of church-produced "products" that they might need here and there—a baptism, a wedding, a funeral, maybe an Easter or Christmas service. Financial comfort—personal and congregational—had led the parishioners in the splendid facade to stifling complacency.

Similar suburban church stories led me early in my ministry to try to tackle the complex relationship between money and ministry. Most of the especially productive suburban ministries that I heard about were not known for their ostentatious buildings.

Meanwhile, some of the most impressive church structures were mere facades for lifeless congregations. Although there were plenty of exceptions in both cases, the relationship between material and spiritual "success" gnawed at my soul. How could financial stewardship become a two-edged sword that blessed some suburban churches and suffocated others?

Biblical Views of Money

Hoping to teach the Corinthians about wise stewardship, Paul told them that the Macedonians had used their material possessions in truly Christian ways. When I preached on this text (2 Cor. 8:1–7) a professional fund-raiser happened to be worshiping with us. After the service he told me that my highly idealistic sermon was the most frank and unvarnished message on giving he had ever heard. I was surprised because I really did not say anything earthshakingly new; I simply relayed Paul's message about the Macedonian churches that "out of the most severe trial" and "extreme poverty" they were so grateful to God that they "gave as much as they were able, and even beyond their ability." In other words, they were not just generous givers, but also joyful givers. Was that idealistic? From a purely earthly or human perspective, probably so. Along the same lines, though, expecting people to do anything out of gratitude rather than duty or self-interest is somewhat idealistic. For example, why should a family that has labored hard to achieve middle-class status give away any of the rewards or blessings that it seemingly has earned? What really should motivate giving? Guilt? Compassion? Gratitude?

Jesus paid attention to wealth because it often threatened the spiritual lives of individuals and congregations. He did not instruct disciples in order to improve their system for money-raising efforts in the church. Instead Jesus sought to keep believers from spending too much time and energy on material things. Money is important, even critical to the operation of the church. At the same time, however, money can become an unhealthy diversion if not a compulsion among Christians. Raising funds and building human testimonies to God-given wealth can weaken the spiritual foundation of churches. The health-and-wealth gospel—that people merely need to claim from God their promised pecuniary prosperity in order to become personally and extravagantly rich—is popular especially in large, growing suburban churches aimed at first-generation middle-class families.

Recognizing the real power of money to motivate people for good and ill, Jesus repositioned money in relation to other, more important things of this world. Jesus needed money. Jesus used money. Jesus respected the persons who shared it. Jesus admired people who administered it carefully and profitably. But Jesus never let material things—mammon—define motive or ministry in the church. Jesus overturned the tables of profiteers at the synagogue, yet the same incarnate God never condemned wealth per se. Instead, he blessed and loved the poor and rich alike as long as they loved God, first, and their neighbors, second, as themselves. In other words, Jesus knew and therefore preached that a person's and church's "treasures" are ultimately matters of the heart; if believers' hearts are collectively filled with gratitude to God rather than self-righteousness, financial problems will tend to solve themselves.

One of my best and wealthiest friends donated huge amounts of money to numerous worthy causes, including the church. He never demanded credit or influence. We were discussing this subject one day, and he said to me, "I feel sorry for people who don't know the joy of giving." Giving is often presented merely as a matter of obligation, not joy. In addition, a lack of giving is associated with sin and guilt, causing people to give for the wrong reason. Giving is a sure road to joyous living regardless of how much individuals and families are able to give away; the widow's mite is just as important as the CEO's tithe; both can be signs of a healthy suburban church, where all blessings are acknowledged as gifts from God.

Planting Stewardship in a New Congregation

What gives any church the power and resources it needs to be the congregation's anchor in life's storms? Not its buildings, wealth, or beauty. Believers, atheists, and everyone else know this. And yet Christians often attest to a church's success by citing physical evidence. In the suburbs, this distorted emphasis on material proof of achievement is increasingly evident in the ways that ministers and the laity alike pridefully extol the "faithfulness" of elaborate ministry "centers" defined by acreage, square footage, seating capacity, the number of parking spaces, and how many volunteers it takes to direct traffic. Often located along highways, many of these behemoth complexes tellingly resemble shopping malls except for the fact that the expansive parking lots are nearly vacant throughout the week. Is that good stewardship? What message does fifty acres of unused asphalt suggest to motorists cruising down the highway?

Nevertheless, the general public does implicitly assess the local church in light of its apparent financial viability as a symbolic expression of "success." For instance, there was a radical change in the attitude of the general public when our fledgling church of five years moved into a new sanctuary on a prominent corner. The structure proved to be a landmark, with its steeple pointing heavenward over a twelve-hundred-seat sanctuary. Dedication Sunday found every seat taken! By normal suburban standards, such a church building would suggest a membership of hundreds of families. But a congregation of only eighty-two families had built the structure in order to serve the spiritual needs of the community. Members had graciously used their money and bank credit to witness publicly to their desire to serve others. We trusted God to show us the way even as we went into debt. Our motive seemed right and fitting, not self-serving. We knew that the structure and grounds would have to be pleasing to the sight of upper-middle-class homeowners in an area where lawns, flower gardens, and designer homes were highly attractive if rarely palatial.

Many area residents had seen our model of the master plan in public buildings and at the nearby shopping mall. They watched the sanctuary take shape on the busy corner. In their view, we were emerging from a tentative, struggling group of church people with some abstract building ideas into what now became an expression of the American idea of success. To some of them, our church was finally worth investigating. We might make an aesthetic if not spiritual contribution to this model village, they thought, applying their common standard of material success to our structure. In a sense, our architectural message had spoken to the residents in their visual vernacular: we are here to serve you *well*, not just to serve you. A strip-mall-like structure could not have conveyed the same message; malls come and go without a sense of permanency, and usually without much concern for the aesthetics of the community.

From inside the congregation, however, we knew that the new building was a humble message of gratefulness. In order to stay on spiritual track, we needed to pledge mutually before God that we would not become "a reed shaken in the wind" of "important people" who wanted to use us. If we were not careful, we could appeal pridefully to those in the community who had the means to deliver us from our debt. They would strip us of our real purpose, vision, and strength in Christ. Money, numbers, size, or notoriety had better not replace our grateful call to servanthood. We were there, in a new structure, to give, to empty ourselves—not to become smug for our own sense of self-satisfaction.

Once again, we determined to keep money, and all of the power and prestige that accompanies it, in its place. Money would not replace our mission! Money would not control our agenda. Money would be our servant on behalf of others. We would accept financial gifts only from those who seemed truly to love God and to want his work to flourish. This desire to be faithful, God-honoring givers and receivers would determine our fund-raising principles and methods of voluntary stewardship. Somehow we would speak *in* the local aesthetic vernacular without becoming a congregation *of* the suburban mammon. Might we have to turn away some financial blessings? Probably so. Could we grow significantly in our upwardly mobile area without being co-opted by the "almighty" dollar? We trusted God to show us the way. We were idealistic as well as faithful.

Starting or renewing a suburban church presents special challenges and opportunities regarding the stewardship of money. Our founding members had faith enough in their call and commitment to underwrite the budget for a sufficient length of time to establish a voluntary support base. New members merely had to accept the fact of ongoing voluntary financial practices without pledging particular amounts. We sought significant but grateful giving, not legalistic formulae for contributions; the latter would easily land us in the same boat as the stone church I admired on my car trip to Iowa. This texture of congregational gratefulness expands the financial base in proportion to the growth pattern; the more we would grow—in theory at least—the more grateful we would become, and the more we would give. We figured that once an adequate voluntary income was established, the congregation would have demonstrated its viability apart from tithing and nonstop fund-raising campaigns pitched from the pulpit. This was indeed our idealism as a new congregation with fewer than a hundred members.

Oddly enough, we were less materialistic than we were biblical dreamers who never really imagined any other way of being financially faithful in the suburbs. Why? Partly because we were nondenominational. We did not have the luxury of a subsidy. But also because we had the advantage of defining our financial practices from scratch, based on enduring biblical principles rather than short-term fund-raising tactics. We assumed that money would never be an excessive burden to a congregation that has a servant heart for the people of the community, combined with a grateful heart that fuels its mission to the world. Faith, self-discipline, and commitment cannot be contrived; they are the results of the Holy Spirit in the hearts of God's people.

Therefore, membership in our new church came with a willingness to join a congregation that thankfully confessed the primacy of Jesus Christ. Any visitors would quickly see that we were cheerful volunteers of financial resources, freely given. They could then discern their own hearts to see if they felt called to join such a community. We church leaders were not there to make new members feel guilty or to strong-arm them into giving. We were called to echo God's gospel of grace so the love of the Lord would overtake them. Then they would want to give even if they did not have the money to give.

Practically speaking, though, we had to make our stance regarding money as explicit as possible to those who desired to join the church. Even if they were easily able to support the church, they might not be ready to do so for the right reasons, with grateful hearts lifted up to their Savior. In our relatively wealthy community, this clearly would become an issue; we could become a way station for misguided givers who simply sought a place to call "my church." So we decided that no one could become a member unless they understood and subscribed to our covenant of faith as defined in our constitution, shared our vision of spiritual service in our community, and witnessed to the record and life of Jesus. No one could buy his or her way into the church.

Turning Away Money

At times our stance regarding money and membership became difficult for some area residents who assumed that our young congregation would be honored if not obligated to have them as members. Some did not especially like our evangelical stand with respect to salvation by grace in Christ alone. Others were a bit uncertain about the implications of our biblical stand on unethical business practices and dishonest use of other people's money. Evidently a few possible new members saw our biblical view of grateful stewardship as a challenge to business practices. But we could not harbor in the name of Jesus those who exploited innocent widows or misrepresented their products or services. We were careful to protect our integrity by not knowingly accepting into full membership those successful suburbanites who hypocritically sought to join a church just to baptize, marry, and bury for purely social reasons. We would rather lose their annual donation than lose our soul.

Communicating this kind of stand was not easy, but we took it very seriously. We regularly held classes for inquirers to explain our biblical beliefs and resulting congregational practices. Such meetings gave community people an opportunity to ask questions about our faith and programs. What nearly always surprised them and received their applause, however, was how we dealt with our financial needs, budgets, mission, and benevolence. Our gospel-centric, gratitude-based approach to giving generally struck sub-urbanites as a refreshing, fitting alternative to guilt-based or duty-driven methods. They knew about money and its effects on people and organizations. By and large, inquirers were prepared to use their money to love others rather than to control them. So they tended to agree with our stand in the first place; our task was to explain the basis for giving, which meant explaining the gospel.

As is usual in Christian congregations, we passed the offering plates at our worship services using only these words: "Let us worship God with our tithes and offerings." No pitches. No guilt trips. No promise about how givers would be blessed in return.

This approach to financial stewardship led many new attendees to ask church leaders exactly the right questions—questions that began to reveal to them the very nature of grace as a free gift that, when truly accepted, generates a heart for giving. The church is a business in the sense that it has to make ends meet and use its resources wisely, but not a business in the sense of mere budgeting.

We never wavered from this approach even though it required regular explanation. As we grew to over 5,400 members we never missed meeting our expenses. For over three decades, we challenged some of the conventional wisdom about suburban church financing. We focused on the quality of ministry, not the effectiveness of fund-raising. And we simply rejected attempts by some misguided people to tell us how to "do it right," which really meant doing it their way. Successful corporate and nonprofit leaders admired our faith-based giving along with our very scrupulous accounting.

Good financial stewardship results from good theology, not from gimmicks. Like all theology it can be taught carefully and even persuasively. The church is the primary institution in the world that can organize itself biblically in order to demonstrate the theological principles of the Christian administration of finances. We tried to apply these principles of grace and giving to suburbia. It was a rewarding as well as challenging experience.

Rewriting the Book on Giving

Before developing our financial program, those of us in the core group, especially the first board members, explored together the biblical basis for grateful volunteerism. First, we concluded that our financial program had to be an integral part of our spiritual ministry. Mature Christians do not see the world or the church as part secular and part Christian, part material and part spiritual. They do not desire to be fairly worldly and fairly godly, but instead to be faithful in all aspects of their lives. A biblical worldview, we concluded, allows for no exceptions to the authority and glory of God. Money is included as *one* aspect of Jesus' lordship.

Second, we discovered that the church ultimately does not depend on money. Money depends on, even serves, the church. Finances do make possible some institutional forms of the church in the world—that is, particular means of organizing, meeting, promoting, educating, and the like. The "church," as the kingdom of God, is the body of followers of Jesus, not any specific buildings or programs. Some congregations can, and do, meet "successfully" in homes without paid staff, let alone property. Decisions about how to organize a particular congregation of Jesus followers are largely cultural practices, not strict ecclesiology. For instance, the principles of good, biblical theology—such as mutual love as well as submission, necessary authority under Christ, and a regard for the sanctity of sacramental administration—can be applied very differently according to cultural context. The church must wisely use its resources within culture, never being controlled by money itself or by various cultural views of money that disrespect its spiritual importance.

Third, money must always be used to accomplish its own, true purpose, its reason for existence, even as adapted to a particular time and place. Since the church serves the larger mission of the kingdom of God, money must serve the programs and persons that aim to love God and neighbor. Sometimes it will be clear how to do this faithfully, such as how to educate children in the faith or to evangelize the nearby neighborhood. Other times this application of resources to programs will be hit or miss even as a learning experience. Stewardship involves *some* measured risk, perhaps especially in suburban cultures that tend to be so fluid. Without applying spiritual meaning to giving, however, applied ministry will be easily corrupted, even turned worldly. For instance, time, too, is a form of capital to be used wisely and well to advance ministry. Often suburban churches look up to members who are big donors but fail to appreciate the sacrificial offerings of time from people of relatively modest means.

Fourth, voluntaristic giving in tune with gratitude seems to suggest that there ought not to be a separate person or committee that determines the financial needs of the congregation. Ministry opportunities should drive finances, not the other way around. Elders, deacons, and trustees ought to be monitoring and evaluating ministry; they should be the most aware of the activities and programs of the church by participating in the "pinch-points" that emerge. They should know where the Spirit is at work, organizing and developing necessary programs to articulate and meet congregational as well as outside needs. The idea of having a financial committee make such decisions on its own, apart from where the Spirit is active, does not fit stewardship.

Fifth, communication is vital to stewardship programs. How can the church, as a steward of resources, function without candid, sincere discussions about its use of funds? If the conversations occur only among congregational leaders, good community stewardship cannot happen. The resulting "us-them" relationship between the leadership and the congregation is lethal. Supportable projects must be clearly defined, recognized, and "owned" by the membership overall, not just by those who are ultimately responsible for setting budgets and disbursing funds.

Without this mutual trust and integrity, we could never have achieved financial as well as spiritual unity. For thirty-one years we actually enjoyed open discussions; enthusiastic, unanimous approvals; and follow-up support for every major financial proposal. Widely recognized needs were always funded, while pet projects could run into trouble. Many members were spiritually enriched by our stewardship approach and testified to their gratitude that this church did not need to talk excessively about money, but gave freely and enthusiastically based on honest, forthright explanations of the needs.

Teaching about Tithing

As senior pastor and preacher, I had a unique entrée to the congregation for recognizing such needs. My responsibility included making visitors comfortable in our Sunday services. I made the special announcements, set the spiritual and worshipful ambiance, and subtly offered our congregation's own story. Knowing the typical suburbanite, but not normally acquainted with the particular individuals who visited, I would describe our parish's intent to serve the community at no cost and without obligation. Our members were their hosts. Visitors were our guests; they should not feel obligated to contribute to the offering.

When membership inquirers came to the final class, I explained to them our method of financing the church. Since our suburbanites were generally observant, educated, creative persons, they recognized the connection between themselves and the financial support of the church. I would speak about tithing in both Old Testament and New Testament terms. But I would add that the law, including tithing, is not only a rule but also a tutor that leads us to Christ. In our new life we find the deep joy of the Holy Spirit. Our values and loyalties should center in God and his redemptive purposes, not merely our own interests. If his work needs money, we should joyfully support it.

Then I would challenge possible members with these thoughts: "If this church is not a blessing to you, it does not deserve your money. Give your own offerings to other Christian causes. But if it is a blessing, give as you are blessed. There are no quotas or even suggestions. You alone can know when you feel right about your contributions."

I encouraged new members to keep in mind that they, too, are responsible for the church's ministry. No one else, beyond the members, is obligated. Christ Church needs part of their tithe. I further explained that their giving would renew their interest in the church. Where their treasure is, their heart would be; and where their hearts were, their treasures would be. The trustees would not come knocking on their doors. New members should strive to be aware of our mutual needs by talking with other members, reading the bulletin, and asking questions.

Then I concluded, "If you have never tithed before I will make you an offer you cannot refuse. I have done this for years, and I know it will give you great joy. Begin to tithe today. If you regret you did so after six months or a year, let me know, and I will see to the return of your money in such a way that no one else will know." This offer was usually met with chuckles. But hundreds accepted the challenge, and I received many reports of the blessings that resulted. No one ever asked for a refund.

Everyone who joined the church for thirty-one years heard this stewardship message. Staff and elders were present at these introductory sessions, which took place between six and ten times annually. Such consistent, repetitive, direct presentations of our governing principles and practices were important. We all knew where we stood as responsible, grateful givers.

We were a suburban church without bake sales, car washes, strawberry festivals, candy peddlers, or magazine subscriptions. We were a congregation that protected people's time so their spiritual as well as family lives could be strengthened and enhanced.

In many cases they could have easily tithed to the church, but many went a step further, serving other members.

Overseeing the Needs

This stewardship approach does not work without clearly established and enforced guidelines for soliciting, managing, and allocating funds. In a large church I attended for years while vacationing, the loose policies and irresponsible practices regarding money split the congregation, caused serious agony for the unsuspecting leaders and staff, and devastated the spiritual lives of many members. I learned that money management is a serious matter well worth careful and prayerful consideration lest it become a major hindrance to the achievement of a church's vision.

Sometimes a major cause would impress elders and other members, so that we felt called to help as good neighbors. In such situations we mobilized ourselves. Suburbanites need spiritual help like everyone else, but they also often have hidden hearts aching with problems as well as with a desire to help, to serve, and to make a difference. For instance, after a year of worshiping at the school there was a growing sense among the members that the gymnasium was not adequate. The congregation itself began asking for a solution to this welcomed problem.

The elders appointed a building committee to confirm the need. At that time, we had given significantly to missions but had not started a building fund. But this situation did not deter the committee from developing a long-range building plan based on a projected growth to three thousand members. We placed the model for the campus plan in a major restaurant, then in a bank lobby, and finally in a nearby hotel. Some who saw the model were intrigued by our optimism. Others asked questions. And still others came to the gymnasium to worship with us on Sunday morning.

Meanwhile, our finance committee met in the home of the chair. We discussed how the funding might be raised and handled. How could we persuade a lending agency to take such a risk with only eighty-two member families? I listened in amazement as these members decided that this was the Lord's work and the money would come. Without blinking, the chairman offered to help and volunteered a major gift. He thought we should all pledge a three-year gift, ask the congregation to help as they could, and then borrow the balance from a bank.

Because it was my first experience with significant volunteer financing, I was unprepared. This was big money to me, especially on a pastor's salary. I felt a bit like one does when stretching uncomfortably to purchase a first home. Yet I wanted to be one with the larger donors. I, too, had already been a grateful giver, not just an employee or the boss. But financially I was just an average member, dependent on others' expertise and gifts. Nevertheless, I witnessed how the meeting affirmed our mutual commitment to ministry in our growing suburb. I was thrilled to participate as a giver as well as the pastor. We took this plan to the trustees, the congregation, and finally to the bank. Were we crazy or farsighted?

Surprise Giving

While we were building with loans, a man who lived a block from the church called. He told me that he was a lifelong member of a denomination and did not intend to leave it. But he had a question. Did we have plans for a church bell? We did. As it turned out, he had grown up hearing church bells. He paid for three solid bronze bells that have rung daily for decades.

When we were about to occupy our building, we had a few primary and nursery rooms to furnish. Lacking money for quality furnishings, I called on a well-wishing villager whose children attended our Sunday school. He had told me that he would like to help us if the occasion ever arose. He provided what we needed.

At one of our trustee meetings we were considering installing only half of the pews in the sanctuary and using the remaining space for Sunday school and educational facilities. At a later meeting we were looking at a sketch of this plan when our secretary said, "My wife and I feel that all the space will be needed for worship. If you decide to install all the pews, we will pay for them in addition to our building pledge."

God spoke clearly that evening. We all knew that this was going to be a need—sooner or later. Yet one courageous person spoke up, and the need was met sooner. We installed all the pews. On dedication Sunday, all of them were filled. Some of us had to admit that at least one of our trustees had a calling that met the size of our need. One year later we needed more space, so we began a second service.

As we grew numerically and spiritually, the giving spirit did not diminish among congregants. At lunch one day I listened to an enthusiastic, successful businessman of our village speak about the blessings of our worship services. I was about to get up to leave when he suddenly asked, "Do we have plans for and know the cost of a pipe organ?" I assured him we had built space for a fine organ. The first installment would be $165,000.

He looked at me and said, "If I give you a check for $65,000, do you think you could find the rest?" I nearly broke into a jig in the restaurant. That evening I got on the phone and began calling members. That night our church secured funding for a pipe organ.

Conclusion

Each year on the Sunday following Thanksgiving, we reported to the congregation a very brief, factual statement about our general fund. I informed them of how much we needed to receive during the month of December to end the operating year in the black. Each week the figure was updated, and on the first Sunday of the New Year I was always able to announce that we achieved our goal. This simple celebration affirmed God's grace and blessing, especially because there was no hype or legalistic statistics about giving averages or quotas. Just joyful givers.

Healthy suburban churches nurture caring, generous habits that result in sufficient volunteers and funding to support their programs. They never treat members as mere fund-raising objects. Nor do they rely on past generations of givers to foot the bills—as occurred in that endowed stone church I admired. Still, genuine needs will have to be carefully communicated to members, just as members have to be encouraged to stay informed about the church's ministries and needs. Along with administrative transparency and integrity, this approach produces trust rather than guilt, and joy rather than cynicism.

Discussion Questions

1. Would it be proper to put the donor's name on a gift to your church? Why or why not?
2. Would it be appropriate to hire professional fund-raisers to conduct a drive for your church? What stewardship principles would be involved in making the decision?
3. Should seminaries teach the principles and practices of financial stewardship? Would you send your pastor and/or other church leaders to such a course? Why or why not?

Chapter Ten

Growing Together in Faith

He was a quintessential American entrepreneur, dreaming dreams, inventing, even selling his own business franchises. He had a well-known Christian family name and proclaimed that he wanted to serve Christ. He described how disappointed he was with believers who lacked the courage of their convictions. He drove a luxury automobile, demonstrated endless energy and self-confidence, and was generous as well as successful.

He and his wife regularly attended worship. Their lovely children actively participated in church school. The couple contracted to buy a home in our village and enrolled their children in the public schools, even paying tuition as a potential resident because he wanted a quality education for his advantaged offspring. His knowledge of the Bible was clear and convincing. When he volunteered to teach, we also discovered his captivating gift of verbal communication. His sense of humor and charismatic personality attracted a large adult class that found new excitement in familiar Bible stories.

He brought our youth group free caramel corn from his stands in neighboring shopping malls. To support our expanding church work, he generously loaned us space in his office building. Although he never became a member, he promised $10,000 annually to our building and general funds. Several members purchased business franchises from him. He personally tipped the scale in favor of the church, borrowing a major sum to build the first structure in our master plan. Everybody at church loved him.

How fortunate we were to have his energy and enthusiasm released in our small, new congregation! Every suburban church plant should pray for more people like him to help build a stable, mature congregation. Right? Wrong!

Superficial Suburban Spirituality

The man described above sounds like the "perfect" church member. Christian faith, however, consists of much more than learning Bible stories, thinking positively, being enthusiastic, and contributing. For instance, despite his generosity, this man suffered from a lack of spiritual integrity. He could talk Christian lingo and labor enthusiastically for the church, but like many successful suburbanites, he lacked a healthy integration of faith and works for the long haul. His bursts of religious activity were not anchored in an ongoing, stable faith in God. In his mind, and probably in his heart, faith was merely one bout of people-pleasing do-goodism after another—not a slow, steady maturation.

This man's explosive influence was like the momentary outburst of a crowd watching an exceptional skyrocket on the Fourth of July—brilliant and exciting for a moment but quickly extinguished. In spite of his promises, he never paid his school tuition bill, wrote the church a bad check for his building commitment, and sold fraudulent business franchises to church members. Soon he and his family disappeared from the village.

Planting the Biblical Vision

As it turned out, our enthusiastic friend was neither a genuine entrepreneur nor a real friend in Christ. His faith was a mere mood, a positive attitude—not sacrificial obedience to God for lifelong service. To stretch the analogy, he was like a fly-by-night strip-mall speculator who builds for short-term profit with no real commitment to the community or to the shop owners. Unlike the self-sacrificing friends described in John 15—friends who, like Jesus, would die for one another—he was only a self-interested partner to himself. His view of the kingdom of God was, at best, short-sighted and superficial and, at worst, a self-delusional gimmick for using others rather than serving them.

The long-range health of suburban churches cannot be measured accurately by short-range numerical growth, flashy building projects, community name recognition, exciting fund-raising campaigns, high-profile members, or any other worldly criteria that give the impression of suburban success. Rather, suburban success has to be measured by the same biblical standard for all times and places: increasingly faithful members who love God, keep his commandments, and love their neighbors as themselves.

Normally a unified congregation characterized by such faithfulness will grow spiritually and numerically, will become more visible in the community, and will earn a good name for itself as a place and people of self-sacrificial love.

Like the early church (Acts 5), we learned dramatically that we were a congregation of sinners called to be better people than we are by nature. As leaders who knew and admitted our own faults in hopes of overcoming them together, we decided to serve and welcome everyone from our community. Anyone could attend our classes and social events. Anyone could receive our pastoral care and counseling. Who were we to be inhospitably elitist or self-righteous? We would simply offer a multitude of programs without cost or obligation to those who came seeking what we had to offer. Our doors, like our hearts, would remain open. In other words, we offered open access to a way of life anchored in sacrificial witness to God's great goodness in Christ.

To become a member of the congregation, however, attendees had to take the step of inquiring, thereby showing us that the Holy Spirit was probably active in their lives. They could not simply enroll, like joining a country club during an open membership period. We did not solicit "members." Instead, we made every effort to offer the gospel by word and deed so others might see and taste the life of faith. Presumably the Spirit-led inquirers would eventually seek the fellowship and wisdom of like-minded people. They would desire a maturity of faith. The leadership of the church is responsible for providing the organizational structure so that this maturity of faith can happen as people are led by the Spirit to pursue it. Along the way, leaders have to guard against compromise or confusion.

A suburb is a busy place. Residents have many activities vying for their time and energy. They select "preferences" among hobbies, neighborhoods, foods, entertainment, and faiths. Without faith anchors, their preferences become more or less selfish—what they *want* but not necessarily what they truly *need*. They approach life as if they were merely hunting for self-satisfying products and services. If a suburban church is not careful, it, too, becomes a congregation of religious "shoppers" who never really get to know their Lord and their spiritual brothers and sisters.

Someone like the enthusiastic fake should be welcomed into the church but not made into a leader or representative of mature faith. In many respects he was a spiritual juvenile who needed discipling; his mistaken approach to work exemplified this as well. We wrongly gave him a leadership position for Bible study instruction before we actually knew him. Soon we corrected this kind of problem by allowing nonmembers to attend, participate, and assist but not to teach or occupy leadership positions until our more mature leaders had time to become acquainted with them and they had become members of our congregation. This change in policy served us well; no one ever questioned it after we had a chance to explain it in new-member classes and other venues.

On the one hand, the biblical vision for the church is highly egalitarian. As the Protestant Reformers put it, the body of Christ is a "priesthood of all believers" who share faith in Jesus Christ. There is a single, "universal" church that includes all who profess faith in Christ regardless of their denominational or congregational church membership, and whether they are Roman Catholic, Protestant, or Orthodox. In addition, there are Christ followers who have yet to join any church even though God is at work in their lives. The Spirit blows where it will.

On the other hand, the church is an organization, founded by Jesus but now in human hands to advance the kingdom of God by using its "keys" to open and close its doors, welcome and admonish, disciple members, and demonstrate mature faithfulness. As Dietrich Bonhoeffer put it, the church cannot survive as a place of "cheap grace" without the cost of God-loving, God-serving, God-pleasing sacrifice.

If the long-gone businessperson had stayed with us, would he have grown enough in his faith to become a more consistent, self-sacrificing witness of Christ in the community? Perhaps so. At the time, we were an immature congregation still discovering our way. Over time we learned how to nurture faithfulness. Yet the question still comes to our minds through new challenges and opportunities. Every suburban congregation has to ask itself repeatedly how it can help suburbanites and their families witness a mature Christian faith to others, so that they desire to become similarly faithful and eventually to take up their responsibilities as worthy though imperfect church leaders? That is our opportunity and challenge.

There are two elements in the historical definitions of faith. The creeds, confessions, and catechisms define faith as *knowledge*, on the one hand, and *action*, on the other. In order to act faithfully, Christians need to grow in the knowledge of the character and attributes of God, the nature of human beings, the redemptive work of Jesus Christ, and the responsibilities of believers to build the church as Jesus commanded. Such knowledge is based on special acts in history through which God revealed these truths and which are recorded in Scripture. As some theologians put it today, the biblical narrative is the "metastory" that sheds light on our everyday lives as fallen but redeemed persons. The church is the trustee of this biblical legacy and has been called to define and organize scriptural truth for her constituents. Christ Church's "Basic Christianity" course was our first effort to teach theology in a popular format. We aimed to instruct new and returning

Christians in the essentials of historic Christian doctrine, precisely because this is generally what is lacking even among believers who know many of the biblical stories.*

Believers who constitute the church "universal," the saints in heaven as well as on earth, have been studying Scripture and earlier studies of Scripture for millennia. They have compiled various basic interpretations and understandings that are foundational to the faith. Throughout church history, faithful Christians have studied the Bible with the guidance of the very Holy Spirit who inspired the biblical writers.

The resulting body of information and wisdom is the precious, indispensable base that should significantly influence the people of God in every time and place. Believers can and should be able to give a reason for their faith, just as believers have had to do from the beginning. This was the rationale for the seriousness with which we pursued educating our people in biblical faith. As we discovered, we could not turn over the task of educating members to anyone who wanted to be a leader. We needed wise teachers intimate with God and his Word as understood by the historic church. We needed to stay away from appointing immature leaders who merely identified with Christian celebrities or who thoughtlessly identified publicly with particular political causes or religious movements.

In our quick-fix society, too many suburban congregations are planted without an adequate definition of the faith they claim to believe and teach. Moreover, as North America becomes increasingly multicultural and complex, believers' ethical and moral choices become similarly difficult to make. While society tries to become more secular in order to accommodate democratic discourse without religious warrants, believers need the capacities to support and defend their Christian choices. As we developed educational programs for our new church plant, we assumed that all of our activities should contribute to the more comprehensive requirement of maturing the knowledgeable faith of our members.

*This course is available in video format at http://www.anatomyofchristianity .org.

The Joy of Learning and Teaching

Contrary to some church-planting theory that implicitly assumes fellowship, fun, and emotional excitement are themselves effective and legitimate goals for church programs, we recognized that all goals have to be anchored in the greater purpose of spiritual maturation. In addition, we discovered that even the deepest Christian education can be conducted in ways that enhance interest and excitement. For example, we witnessed immediate and enthusiastic response to well-conducted biblical studies. Suburbanites are accustomed to investigating matters of interest and concern. We offered the "Basic Christianity" course without any pressure to join the church or even to accept the teachings. We did so without announcements about other activities or follow-up visits by mail or telephone, without any cost or obligation, without expecting a previous knowledge of the Bible or church jargon, and without registering names and telephone numbers. And the people came—all ages and backgrounds. During our early years, we especially accommodated residents' schedules, offering classes at fitting times of day, in convenient locations. These basic classes attracted as few as ten and as many as 150 attendees.

We were stunned by the interest of teenagers. Since I was the only pastor, I led mid-week teen meetings. We held the first session at a home of one of the young people. After a mixer game, we sat in a circle on the floor in a recreation room to get acquainted. My only agenda for the evening was to find out why these youth had come.

When I finally found an opening in the lively conversation, I asked if they had ever attended similar church meetings. A few responded affirmatively. I asked what they did at those meetings. They played games, both inside and outside—things like scavenger hunts, bowling, sports, movies, and parties. I built up my courage, feared the worst, and asked, "What would you like to do if we meet regularly?" Silence. More silence. They began looking at each other and shuffling uneasily, as if embarrassed. Finally, one hand went up sheepishly. I had never seen this person before and had no clues about her personal interests or existing faith commitment. Finally, she said tentatively, "Could we study the Bible?"

The elders and I soon discovered the depth of concern suburban teenagers have about the moral and spiritual choices they must make daily. To adequately care for these people is to lead them to biblical competence and spiritual maturity, not to mere fun and games. Of course, the church had little time to help its youth mature in their faith before they would leave for college and independence—the period when most young suburbanites face very difficult challenges and often compromise their faith. We needed to develop an effective youth ministry that was more than just entertainment. And we needed to instruct parents in the faith so they could be spiritually mature and involved role models for their children.

Teaching Faith in Action

With the help of our new staff, we explored what it would mean to teach spiritual maturity. Humans intuitively have opinions about maturity. Most people agree that maturity is good, and that mature people are worth looking up to because they are more composed and secure, enjoy self-respect, and rise above the negative circumstances of life.

What about spiritual maturity? For biblical and theological knowledge to benefit the church and its members, it must be applicable to life; it must be something that we can seek to "be" and "do." Yet if it is excessively practical, mature action might lose its connection to biblical wisdom. Sometimes churches teach suburban young people so dogmatically that the youth are ill prepared to apply biblical wisdom discerningly to new contexts that invariably come upon them in a complicated world of affluence, choice, and change.

Christians go through a developmental process whereby their faith grows according to a pattern that can lead to spiritual maturity. Christians anchor their morality, for instance, in the nature of God, whose image they reflect. God is believers' unchangeable standard, unaffected by time or culture. He is the one perfect being. With others' help, I discovered a parallel between spiritual development and the stages of moral development. Both address ideals and principles, on the one hand, and actions, on the other.

If a church truly desires to nurture loyal and mature disciples of Jesus Christ, it must build educational programs with both of these goals in mind. The church must teach and model "practical wisdom" or applied knowledge. Some church members are children of the covenant who are already being educated in faith and life within their Christian families, congregations, and schools. Of course, the youth might be learning Christian "behavior" without the underlying knowledge, and vice versa. Other children come to church from homes with minimal, if any, spiritual disciplines.

Adults are similarly diverse in background and needs. They are not all parents. Some have very elementary knowledge of Scripture; others have none; and others have learned extensively about the Bible almost from birth. Adults have extremely diverse spiritual disciplines; some have never even heard the word "discipline" applied to spiritual growth and life. Our budding congregation was poorly equipped to deal with such diversity and needed to lay the foundations of educational programs with great care; otherwise, members might find the instruction overly theological, overly practical, or the opposite. Simply put, they might become bored or indifferent.

Yet reason and logic would not suffice in our planning and instruction. We needed to reach hearts, to inspire wisdom-seeking aimed at wanting to be like Jesus. To accomplish this kind of motivational instruction, we had to teach with and by the Spirit. In other words, our faith-nurturing, faith-building programs had to open learners' hearts and minds to the truth. For Christians, this heart-and-head truth comes by special revelation from God and has been made known in Jesus Christ (John 1:1–14).

All human theorizing is imperfect, but we discerningly used one of the major theories of moral development to help us in our ministry.* This theory described moral development along

---

*Laurence Kohlberg, *The Philosophy of Moral Development: Moral Stages and the Idea of Justice* (New York: HarperCollins, 1981).

several stages—from reward and punishment in early childhood, to experimentation among teens, and eventually to conscience among more mature adults. Being sinners, we humans participate to varying degrees in each stage as we struggle through each one in an effort to develop our faith-based knowledge and actions.

For Christians, the highest stage of maturity is deep knowledge of God and God's Word, coupled with a more practical ability to apply this God-breathed knowledge to our interactions with others in God's world. Our developed "conscience" is no less than deep and wide hearts for loving God and our neighbors as ourselves. Church leaders are responsible for doing their utmost so that every member of the congregation has the opportunity to reach this most profound and satisfying level of maturity, where they are free to live for Jesus Christ as members of a congregation with shared faith. In other words, the church as the very body of Christ shares a Spirit-generated "conscience" that can be informed by biblical truth and result in biblical action. Everything church leaders do, but especially education, must aim toward this worthy end of genuine, informed faith.

Since I was the preaching pastor, I made every effort to help achieve that goal. I had to assume that there would be those in the congregation representing each of the stages of spiritual maturity. Sermons had to reach them all. I had to present the biblical text relevantly, not just as history or abstract principles. The text had to be understood by children and adults and even those already at the highest level of spiritual maturity. If sermons were too simplistic, I would not help them, and probably would lose them. Thankfully, the gospel is both simple and profound, so I could embrace both aspects in the pulpit.

People tend to reach up to a higher stage and not to be inspired by messages at a lower stage of spiritual maturity. This might be especially true among educated, high-achieving suburbanites. But nearly all adults do not like to be treated like children, mentally or spiritually. They prefer to be respectfully challenged.

All of our teaching, social activities, publications, guest speakers, news releases, and counseling were more effective when we considered in advance the likely spiritual maturity of the audiences. The stages of moral-spiritual development provided a benchmark for different internal groups, so that we could always consider how well we seemed to be moving the members and friends of our church family forward toward maturity.

In a young, growing church, programs multiply and often change. Our leaders, boards, and committees found it highly profitable and helpful to ask growth-related spiritual questions in advance of launching or assessing new initiatives:

> How does it help mature our members?
> Is it compatible with our theology and aimed at knowledge and wisdom?
> Do we have the proper mature leadership for excellence?
> Is it repetitious or conflicting?
> Is it the right time?
> Do other institutions provide it?
> Can we afford it?

These and other questions enabled us to create a long-range plan that served as a grid against which we could evaluate church growth programs. We learned early on not to adopt one church program after another simply because they were popular, were peddled by Christian celebrities, or were well promoted. Many of these faddish programs come and go without making any lasting contribution to the spiritual maturity of congregations.

Praying for Spiritual Maturity

Since our church was founded in response to the prayers of God's people, prayer continued to be the congregation's lifeline. We wanted all of our members and friends to be prayer partners—to pray for one another as well as others. From the initial week of our existence, a weekly prayer meeting was our first regular gathering apart from worship. It helped us share and nurture our personal faith. It also helped leaders to assess the spiritual maturity of attendees.

When I was still able to know all of our church families personally, I could match their needs and interests in groups for constructive developmental relationships. This was critically important when we launched a congregational prayer program. To assist in developing the disciplines of personal, family, and public prayer, and to help those who never prayed audibly and felt uncomfortably threatened by it, we offered a "Triads of Prayer" program. We announced that the program would help members become better acquainted, make us all more sensitive to one anothers' needs, and unite us as a church family in daily prayer to God. We leaders promised that prayer would strengthen and enrich us by the power of the Holy Spirit. It did exactly that. Many of these prayer-based friendships continued for decades.

The program began when I preached a sermon on "The Lifeline of the Church" and invited the congregation to consider praying for another person or family for the entire new year. Singles and families could participate by filling in a card from the pew rack during the next two weeks. Leaders would identify three-person partnerships, and each signatory would receive a letter listing the partners. Staff made these assignments based on compatibility and possible spiritual development. Each partner would be asked to pray for one other signatory. For one year, person A would pray for person B, B would pray for C, and C for A. Guidelines called for get-acquainted meetings, explained how to be helpful regarding prayer needs, and cautioned against prying into each other's lives, wasting others' time, and being a nuisance to partners. They encouraged partners to respect others' time and confidential matters, and to pray daily for them, believing that the Lord would bless them.

God blessed the Triads of Prayer far beyond our ambitious expectations. I still hear about the relationships that that program initiated and the spiritual blessings that continue to this day. Patterns of personal and family prayers that began back then are now regular practice in the lives and homes of many. The indirect blessings have been especially notable. One intergenerational triad began dining together and eventually formed permanent, confidential friendships for mutual guidance and support. A newlywed was able to attend college because her family participated in Triads of Prayer many years ago.

We also moved God's people along the path toward maturity by exposing them to living examples of faithful Christians. Not all of God's saints lived in the past, isolated from modern society. They can be found today in all walks of life, on every continent on earth. Hundreds of them came to Christ Church to tell their stories. They were physicians, lawyers, actors, authors, teachers, artists, musicians, sports figures, business leaders, salesmen, missionaries, statesmen, students, military personnel, politicians, and clergy. They spoke at our couples' club, youth programs, lecture series, mission festivals, retreats, pulpit interviews, Sunday school, breakfasts, debates, and at a variety of special events.

Today North Americans desperately need faithful heroes worth admiring and even imitating. We are destroying former heroes by focusing too strongly on their weaknesses. At the same time, the media tend to expose every flaw in those who are emerging, especially religious, leaders. As a result, we all tend to doubt the integrity of our leaders as though they must be guilty until proven innocent. Meanwhile, our mediated culture frequently turns heroes into money barons who appear to be heroic just for the sake of wealth. Although no humans are perfect, the church always has its selfless saints who serve others out of humble gratitude to God. These people are truly worth imitating because of their spiritual maturity.

We all need to rub shoulders with humble servants of Jesus, observing their ways, learning their motives, and gratefully living as they do. The apostle Paul repeatedly asked new Christians to imitate him not because he was perfect but because the Spirit was active in his life, equipping him to demonstrate and teach about the fruit of the Spirit. Churches can invite saints to their communities of faith, so adults and children alike can catch a vision of godliness in our time.

Authentic Christian leaders do not demand first-class airfares or outrageous speaking fees to serve a church in this manner. Some of our greatest faith heroes came from small beginnings and themselves met a hero in an unexpected place and time. I can testify to the influence of virtuous role models throughout my childhood, including those who influenced me in a seemingly passing and momentary way. I still cherish new, faithful friends that God is sending my way. They yet move me toward more mature Christian wisdom and action. They teach by modeling, not just by professing.

Discipling Creatively

Since growing in the faith is ultimately a matter of discipling, our leaders aimed to cultivate creative ways and means of fostering discipleship for the spiritual benefit of the suburban congregation. I have increasingly realized how indebted I am—and the whole church is—to various associates for their creative dedication to their areas of expertise.

Our education minister, for instance, was always probing for new ways to reach people with Scripture. While I was just beginning to read about the advent of the computer and its potential use in the marketplace, he was already projecting its use for our Sunday school children. Consequently, we developed our own software to help use computers to teach biblical material. Children came early to classes and stood in line to watch the Bible stories unfold on the computer screen as they pushed the magic keyboard. When they told their public or Christian school classmates on Monday morning about their Sunday lessons, our church's reputation with these children took a giant stride. We never jumped into new pedagogies or technologies just to be trendsetters, but neither did we overlook opportunities to improve our methods.

We offered what might have seemed to outsiders like the typical Bible study groups for young adults, women's circles, men's forums, and young men's society—all normally held at church. But in these and other groups we tried to be relational as well as knowledgeable. If we heard or read about a new opportunity for more personal spiritual growth, we would study it, assess its appropriateness for our church, and then sometimes adopt it. For instance, we introduced "Acorn Groups" that met in homes strategically located in the areas where members lived. Volunteer leaders reviewed the study materials with our minister of education and taught as needed in their own neighborhood or elsewhere. Home groups, less formal and official, attracted many membership inquirers, and dozens of them brought hundreds of spiritually open people to our church.

Making the Old New

We also searched for traditional spiritual practices that have escaped modern attention. Having been nurtured in a Reformed (Calvinistic) world-and-life view along with its fairly limited liturgy, I risked a radical departure by introducing healing services. This resulted from several unrelated experiences of miraculous healings along with my own eighteen months of intermittent travel, study, and research. After all, healing has been part of the church since New Testament times. Such healing does not have to be private as long as it is done appropriately with humble faith and without the histrionics that often accompany televised healing crusades. We simply invited all of those in our church and community who needed spiritual, relational, or physical healing to gather in our sanctuary one Sunday evening each month to pray for healing.

The healing service fixed attendees' eyes on Jesus the healer, not on the pastor. It included singing appropriate experiential hymns, a confession of faith, a New Testament Scripture lesson with a brief exposition, preparatory prayer, and the invitation to come forward. All those seeking healing were asked to write their request briefly on a card and present it to the serving pastor or elder. Three or four of us would spread out in the chancel, review every request, and kneel in prayer with each supplicant as she or he came forward.

Prayer services were quiet, respectful of confidentiality, and supported by appropriate organ music. We defined each service as a quiet time and place near to the heart of God, who desires to heal all human brokenness and who promises that by faith all believers will one day be made fully new, physically as well as emotionally and spiritually. Our simple services were inspired by biblical practices that have been maintained largely by Anglican and Roman Catholic practices. These services were immediately accepted, and there were many healings of relationships as well as of bodies and souls. Also, we never used the positive results of these services to prompt attendance at future services or to convince attendees to expect miracles. We simply drew near to God, and he drew near to us, as is promised in the book of James.

Conclusion

While Christian maturity depends on the gift of the Holy Spirit and sound biblical and theological understanding, it usually develops when congregational leaders learn to address creatively the diverse spiritual needs represented in a congregation. Suburban congregations are varied, each in their own way, even if they do not seem as heterogeneous as churches in transitional urban neighborhoods, on college campuses, or on some multicultural mission fields. Suburban congregational diversity often reflects a wide range of Christian and non-Christian backgrounds, an amazing scope of knowledge and ignorance about the Bible and basic Christian doctrine, and sometimes wildly different notions about what it means to live faithfully.

For Christ Church's children, we devised a master plan so that those attending our Sunday school would learn a selected number of Bible texts and stories, hymns, and even creedal statements by the time they might make their public confession of faith as young adults. During these same years, the youth and mission departments would teach, guide, and counsel them in developmental experiences. We sought for them to learn how to "know" and "do" Christianity—how to know God and his Word, and how to act wisely on that knowledge.

Where did the fake entrepreneur go wrong? How did he learn to promise so much and deliver so little to others? Somewhere along the line he probably learned to sell a facade rather than give his broken self in the service of others. He sold himself short because his vision of the kingdom was far too tiny. He figured out how to pitch an image without substance, all the while convincing himself that he needed only himself to be successful in life. True faithfulness is much more than self-interest, as suburbanites need to hear. After all, it is relatively easy to grow up comfortably in suburban "islands" of spiritual superficiality, stuck in the first few stages of moral and spiritual development. But the triune God is there, in the hearts, minds, and actions of faithful followers, whose missional lives point to a more fruitful and more mature way of life.

Discussion Questions

1. How would you describe your personal room to spiritual maturity? How close are you to your own spiritual goals?
2. What characteristics identify a Christian person who has gained enough spiritual maturity to leave home for college or employment? How well is your church equipping such members?
3. What is the chief motivation that should drive a Christian person and congregation to spiritual maturity?